'I am a psychologist in practice for 30 years, and this is the most cogent and wise approach I've encountered to date. It's the only approach I've seen that combines all aspects of this complex problem: neurochemistry, blood sugar, nutrition, the rebelliousness of the human spirit, and the power of intentional mindfulness into a practical, sensible plan for altering those addictive neural pathways.'
April Martin, PhD

'This book changed my life. Most importantly I am able to integrate all this into my normal daily living. I do not have to say no to parties or social gatherings afraid I will break my diet! This is a lifelong, liveable way of relating to food.'
Dr Rosaire O' Donovan

'This is an awesome book. Concrete and do-able, it's ground-breaking advice. Makes me feel I don't need to fall out of love with food, or disconnect myself from it, rather that I can turn my passion from a negative to a positive one. Really exciting stuff. I have spent so much of my life with my head in the sand because I thought nothing would ever work.

Having read your book Eating Less, I think this more condensed format actually gives the message a lot more punch. I feel energised and able after reading this. The ease of the read somehow syncs with ease of attitude I'm searching for. This is more compelling than ever.'
Amy Marshall

'I can't even remember the last time I had a huge blow out binge to the point of discomfort and pain. I can now comfortably leave food on my plate without worrying about it. I can now socialise without feeling stressed and anxious. Before, I was an all day grazer and any little graze could trigger a major big binge and that was the day in tatters.

My husband comme ... s recently that I'm ... relaxed and less uptight. I think ... d life in general.'
Naomi Cresswell

DITCHING
DIETS

HOW TO LOSE WEIGHT
IN A WAY YOU CAN MAINTAIN

Gillian Riley

Full Stop

eatingless.com

CONTENTS

Introduction: Three questions   *How to eat less without following a diet. Everything you need, summed up in three themes.*   **page 1**

Chapter 1: Am I choosing?   *You're being 'good' while you stick to the rules, but then you're 'bad' and return to overeating. The solution is to learn how to eat less through a genuine sense of free choice – rather than prohibition.*   **page 9**

Chapter 2: Why does it matter to me?   *Strengthen your motivation with feedback that's immediate and more lasting than weight loss alone.*   **page 23**

Chapter 3: How am I dealing with temptation?   *Instead of trying to avoid your interest in food you don't need, which can't possibly work forever, discover how to overcome it by thinking in a completely new way.*
                    page 37

Chapter 4: How to get a new brain   *Understand a few things about what happens in your brain when you want to overeat, and you can work with your brain instead of against it.*   **page 57**

Chapter 5: Why you eat so much   *It will help you to lighten the impact of all the meanings, explanations and stories that support your overeating.*   **page 73**

Chapter 6: Give yourself a break   *Learn how to eat in an imperfect way, so that a few bad choices don't turn into an ongoing disaster.*   **page 85**

Chapter 7: Good food and bad food   *It's important to know that some food enhances your health and some undermines it. You can discover the difference – and still not turn that into a rule you've got to follow.*   **page 101**

Chapter 8: Putting it all together   *How to live in a world full of food temptations, continue to eat less of them and feel at peace with yourself about that.*

page 111

Further Help   *A variety of resources are available if you want support to go further with this approach.*

page 121

References   *A selection of published research to support everything in this book, together with brief descriptions of the findings in each study.*   **page 123**

INTRODUCTION
THREE QUESTIONS

Welcome to an extraordinary journey. This will be an adventure, and just like all adventures it will be challenging, risky and full of surprises. At times you might think you'll never get anywhere and that nothing will ever change. At other times you might fear so much will change you won't be able to handle it. Just stay with it and watch what happens. Let those thoughts and fears come and go. Get some support with it if you want to, someone to talk to about it all. I know you want something to change; otherwise you wouldn't be reading this book in the first place. So in a sense you've already started the journey. Just don't give up on it, however long it takes, and you will get there in the end.

First things first. You want to change something about the way you are with food, so that you can be more in control of what you eat. Now, in order to change your actions, you change the way you think. Why? Because behind every action there's always a thought. The thought can be ever so subtle, so subtle you may not even notice it, but it's there. You think, 'Another slice of cake looks good' and before you know it you've eaten it. What you can do here is to learn a new way of thinking so that you can change your actions. Then, you have the opportunity not to eat that other slice of cake.

There are, of course, some theories out there that propose biological causes, such as low blood sugar, a lack of amino acids, or other nutrient deficiencies. But research has shown that serious overeating, even in those diagnosed with 'Binge Eating Disorder', responds dramatically to placebo intervention. Although unlikely to be a long-term solution, the fact that this happens at all shows us the significance of the ways in which we think: our attitudes and expectations. (1)

Appetite hormones such as leptin and ghrelin are also highly susceptible to the placebo effect. Providing signals of hunger and fullness, they have a major influence on how much you eat, and the fact that they are strongly influenced by mental expectation is often ignored. (2, 3)

It's not that there isn't also a physical and biological side to all this, it's just that changing the way you think is an extraordinarily powerful factor.

When it comes to changing the way you think about food, there are three things to keep in mind. Let's call them themes. I'm going to describe what they are, so you can understand and remember them. Then, if your eating is not what you would like it to be – you're eating in ways that you later regret – you ask yourself about these three themes.

What you'll discover is that whenever any one of these themes is out of place, you'll feel out of control with food in some way. You'll be eating too much, too often, the wrong things or at the wrong times. When you question and find the truth about these themes for yourself, then you'll feel in control of your eating. Then, you feel at peace with food. Then, you have a good relationship with food and eat in ways you don't regret.

So what are the three themes? I'll list them here and then I'll go into more detail over the following chapters:

1. AM I CHOOSING? Most people deny choice in an attempt to cut back on their eating, whether or not they are actually managing to cut back. If you ever notice a rebellious quality to your eating, especially if you feel completely out of control at times, feeling overwhelmed by intense and persistent cravings, this is the theme for you to tackle. If you keep procrastinating, putting off making good changes or if you feel deprived when you don't eat something yummy, this is the theme for you. When you eliminate these problems, then you take control. You take control by developing a deep sense of free choice.

Only then can you make genuine choices that work for you, choices you really do want to live with.

2. WHY DOES IT MATTER TO ME? Here we look at why you might make one choice over any other. For example, you might ask yourself, 'Why don't I eat some more cake?' Or, 'Why am I snacking on an apple instead of a bar of chocolate?' We always have reasons for the things we do but often we lose sight of what they are, and this is important when it comes to making lasting changes in what you're eating on a regular basis. In Chapter Two we'll see how your motivation can be made much more powerful and sustainable.

3. HOW AM I DEALING WITH TEMPTATION? This theme addresses your desire to overeat; the urge, impulse and attraction towards all that food you don't really need. In the past you may have tried to control this by avoiding temptation or distracting yourself. But it's impossible to keep that up forever, so your success gets compromised. You can begin to think differently about feeling tempted and about feeling satisfied. When you do, things really start to change. This book shows you how.

Is it really this simple? Well, yes and no. It is simple in that all you need to remember are these three themes. It isn't simple in that you need to be honest with yourself so that you don't deceive yourself with false answers. A counsellor – anyone who can listen to you in a supportive way and give you honest feedback about the ideas in this book – can help.

This is about how to make a shift in your thinking that will last, and once you've made that shift you'll never need to diet again. It takes time, effort and courage to change the way you think, but it really is possible.

You can go as fast or as slow as you like. And it isn't necessary to believe in it in order for it to work.

WHAT YOU CAN DO

▸ Do it yourself. Over the next few chapters you'll see how to develop a powerful and very practical sense of choice about food. When you start practising with these ideas, it's best to do it by yourself as much as you can. Think about this by yourself, without trying to get anyone else to help you.

Talking to a counsellor, support person or support group is fine, but as much as possible keep all your discussions about eating and weight within those designated meetings and conversations.

This advice goes double if you have someone in your life who puts any pressure on you to control your overeating and lose weight. If there's someone who makes comments about your size or comments on what you eat, that is especially the person you don't want to get involved in what you're learning here. They may well continue to make their comments but you don't have to respond to them, so don't take the bait and try to change the subject whenever you can.

▸ Of course you'll need to make some decisions with others sometimes: what the family will have for dinner, perhaps, or what restaurant your group of friends will go to. But exactly what and how much you eat is up to you and is best decided by you. So, for example, if you want a second helping of something, you don't talk about it. You learn how to think it through for yourself and make a private decision about whether or not to have it.

Later on, when you've spent a while working with this book, you may want to talk about some of it with people close to you. You'll know when you're ready to do that, and you'll know by then that it's still best not to talk about it when you are eating.

▸ Keep it simple.   One of the best things about this approach is that you don't need to make other changes in your daily life in order for this to work. Learning how to eat less doesn't depend on whether you have a wildly exciting social life or are lonely and isolated. It doesn't depend on whether you're standing up, sitting down, watching TV or reading. It doesn't depend on whether you're at work or at home. Unemployed or bringing up children. Happy and productive or depressed and bored.

You can learn how to control what and how much you eat no matter what is going on in your life. And the best thing about this is that you don't need to wait until other things in your life change before you can make changes in your eating. You can get to work on it right way, just as things are.

In fact, working on things just as they are right now is the best way to proceed. You'll see why later on.

▸ Let it in. The first time you read this book you'll begin to understand the principles, but you'll only get good results if you can let these ideas become real to you. It may take reading this book a couple of times before it sinks in enough to make a difference. This doesn't mean you're a slow learner or that you will never learn anything here that will make a real difference. It's just the way it is for many people. It takes a while, and this means you need to be a bit persistent. First of all you understand these themes, and then you start to live them by bringing them into the daily thoughts you have about food.

It's possible you'll come across some unusual ideas that are completely different to anything you've heard before. It may take a while before you can really let it in.

Take it at your own pace. Keep returning to this book, and eventually you'll be able to own it in a way that enables you to break through the barriers and access the power in you to take control.

Then, things will change. Not just for a while, but in real, lasting ways. Not because you read a book but because you changed the way you think about food.

GILLIAN'S STORY

My own progress with food has been gradual over a number of years, not too dramatic but none the less valuable. I certainly eat a good deal less than I used to and the quality of what I eat has improved beyond recognition. I've made these changes in exactly the ways I describe in this book. I know I really do have the potential to be overindulgent with food. I enjoy my food very much - but I also really enjoy being able to eat less.

People often want to know, so I'll tell you that at my largest I was a UK dress size 18, and now I've been a steady and happy 12 for many years.

Every time I lead a seminar I meet a new group, and as we talk these things through I've learned more about what people need to understand so that eating less can become a natural part of their life. This book contains the experiences, the questions and the answers that have come out of this process.

There's always a wide range of difficulties because everybody's different, but there are also themes I notice over and over again. The effectiveness of addressing these particular themes is supported by scientific research, and that can give you real confidence in the material in this book.

Some of my clients have contributed their comments at the ends of the chapters that follow. It may help you to see these ideas expressed in other people's words.

CHAPTER ONE
AM I CHOOSING?

Whenever you think about limiting what you eat, what kinds of things do you say to yourself? Do you think anything like this?

'I mustn't eat between meals.'
'I've got to stop eating all this bread.'
'I can't eat anything with sugar.'
'I'm not allowed to eat wheat.'
'Don't you dare eat any more of those.'

This style of thinking is very common so I wouldn't be at all surprised if these thoughts or something like them go through your head whenever you try to control your eating. Sometimes they flash by very quickly, so it takes some attention to catch them and realise that this is how you are trying to stop eating so much.

Some people, though, gave up any attempt to control themselves so long ago they've banished these thoughts completely and just go ahead and eat anything they want. If this is so for you, it might be that you could spot this style of thinking *after* you've been overeating:

'I've got to stop eating so much.'
'I shouldn't eat so much junk food/fried food/bread.'
'I won't allow myself any chocolate for the rest of the week.'
'I must start that diet tomorrow.'
'I can't go on like this.'

Most people try to control their eating by thinking in terms of prohibition: commands, restrictions and maybe even threats. They think like an authority figure, a stern parent inside their own heads, shouting out orders. The harder they try, the more urgently this voice shouts at them, judges them and tries to bully them into submission.

   This is what most people think of as willpower. It's no wonder they say they don't have any! I know I wouldn't want any of that. It sounds like a nightmare to me. In fact, it isn't willpower. It's the opposite of willpower and that's why it doesn't work. And it doesn't work, does it? If it did, you'd be out there obeying the orders, always being 'good', following the rules, never overeating or eating anything that's bad for you. The reality is more likely to be that the more you try to restrict yourself, the more you rebel and eat even more. (4)

   You might be one of those people who can go along

with the rules for a while, perhaps when you're on a diet or attending a slimming club. You think, 'I am allowed to eat these things' (whatever is on the diet) and 'I'm not allowed to eat those things' (maybe just a few but not a lot of those things because they aren't on the diet).

It works for a while but you know from experience that it doesn't last. At some point it all falls apart. Rebellious, out of control overeating kicks in again, you're eating even more than when you first started, and you keep putting off returning to the diet because it feels so restrictive. You think, 'I'll do that diet again one day, but not today. I'm too busy to think about it right now'. And so you go on, wishing you had some control with food.

You see, the problem comes from thinking in terms of following rules and restrictions. Thinking this way creates a devastating attitude, which undermines your best intentions. This is the sense of deprivation, which will destroy your attempts to control what you eat. (5)

Feelings of deprivation are an adult version of the temper tantrum a child throws when they want something and are being prevented from getting it. This temper tantrum means you're going to be upset until you get what you want. Maybe you don't go quite as far as throwing tantrums over food, but see if you don't throw a sophisticated, ever so subtle, adult version. An adult version in your head, which can be just as manipulative as the tantrums you see in the supermarkets from the kids with their exasperated mothers.

These deprivation tantrums can be so fleeting they're gone in a second. It can be the briefest glimpse of martyrdom, just at the thought of not eating this particular item you fancy. This feeling is so negative, it need do no more than threaten to appear. This threat is the fear that if you don't eat this thing *now* you're really going to regret it. If you deny yourself this thing, you aren't going to stop thinking about it, you'll eat something else that's even worse to compensate, and when you do get you hands on some you'll eat ten times as many. You've got yourself over a barrel. You're damned if you do – but you're even more damned if you don't.

This is the nightmare so many people live with. They want to eat less, and especially less of certain things, but when they feel attracted to these foods their willpower is nowhere to be found. It's been wiped out by that sense of deprivation, even by the threat of it. And for those people who do manage to struggle through a few days, weeks or months of 'denying themselves', they can feel stressed, depressed and completely obsessed with food.

It could be that what I'm describing here is a fairly simple issue for you to work through, or it can be a major challenge. Often, people who really did have a dictatorial authority figure in their youth take on this style of thinking and can apply it to almost anything in life. (6)

No matter where you begin, when you reduce or eliminate this sense of deprivation, you get to access your ability to take control. You get to eat less in a way that brings you joy and a sense of achievement instead of resentment, misery and, sooner or later, 'cheating' and rebellious overeating again.

I realise you can only take my word for it at this point because you don't have your own experience to test this out yet, but what I want to explain to you in this chapter is that all this difficulty is created by a state of mind. The sense that eating less means you are 'depriving yourself' is nothing but an attitude, a way of thinking. All of that difficulty and negativity is created when you deny your freedom of choice, and you do that by thinking in terms of commands, threats, rules, restrictions and prohibition.

Check out those sentences at the beginning of this chapter and see if any of them don't ever flip through your head. They leave you feeling like you're being bullied. Like you've been locked up, forced to eat rabbit food and there's no way out. (7)

Loss of freedom is surely one of the most devastating things that can ever happen to a human being. This is true of any freedom that's rightfully yours: freedom of speech, for example, the right to vote and the right to worship. These and many more are all freedoms most of us take for granted, and we would object strongly if they were ever taken away. We also have every right to eat whatever is ours to eat – and that's the freedom you deny when you think in terms of 'can't', 'have to', 'not allowed' and 'must'.

The solution is contained in your power of choice. But before you can genuinely choose, you need to know that genuine choices exist. This means acknowledging that you're completely free to eat anything and everything you can get your hands on. I'm not encouraging you to do that. What I'm saying is that by knowing you are free to overeat – *even to eat in ways that could impair your health and wellbeing* – knowing this first of all is what creates a genuine and deep sense of choice. You cannot make real choices unless you first recognize that real options are in fact available.

Let's say you give a substantial amount of money to someone. Compare how you'd feel if the same person stole the same amount from you. In both cases, that money has ended up with the same person; the difference is whether you had a choice about it. If the money had been stolen, you'd be a victim – and you'd feel like one too, wouldn't you? In some sense, that's how you feel while you deny your freedom to overeat – and to continue to overeat.

This denial of choice can live with you for years, even decades. But as soon as you begin to think in a different way, things begin to change, and everything falls in place behind that. You stay in touch with the idea that you are totally free to eat anything you want, as much of it as you want, any time. Then, you'll be able to eat less without feeling deprived, and without any need to rebel. You'll find you have a far greater sense of control – and even liberation.

It's very straightforward and it turns everything on its head. Free choice. The rule is there are no rules. All you need to do is get used to thinking in this new way.

You may, however, already be aware of a fear about this, and this fear can block your path. This fear is that if you really let yourself believe you're completely free to overeat – you will! That's why you deny choice in the first place, because you hope that if you give yourself rules you might obey them, at least for a while. It can take time to overcome this fear, to throw out the rules and let in a stronger sense of freedom around food. It will take developing trust in yourself to make the choices you really do want to live with. That's something that can take time, and it's something that will take more themes we'll be covering later in this book.

It will help you a great deal to fully own the choices you make by choosing the complete picture: not just the enjoyable experience of eating that particular food, but also the way you would expect to feel after you've eaten it. We'll get into that later on.

Are you thinking you've heard all this before? I've often come across advice about making sure you don't deprive yourself of anything, so it's possible this is sounding a bit familiar. The advice I'm talking about is 'to eat whatever kind of food you want but in moderation', and the idea is that then you won't feel deprived. That's not what I'm saying here, and it is very important to understand the difference.

Perhaps you're already aware of the flaw in this common advice. Setting out 'to eat what you want in moderation' is all very well unless eating in moderation leaves you feeling deprived! After all, it is the immoderate amount you eat that you're trying to control in the first place, isn't it? The problem is that eating enough to never feel deprived means overeating, and especially it means overeating things that are aren't so good for your health.

It's likely you think being free to overeat means overeating. In other words, thinking, 'I'm free to eat everything' is the same as, 'I'm going to go ahead and eat everything.' Many people assert their freedom of choice about food by actually overeating. What follows is that even thinking about eating less inevitably feels like restriction, coercion and punishment. And this leads to feelings of deprivation: denial, stress, loss of motivation, attachment to some very compelling excuses, persistent cravings, and then a return to overeating. (8)

There's absolutely no need to go ahead and overeat in order to prove that you're free to. In fact, trying to gain a sense of freedom around food by overeating can be completely counterproductive. This is because you can become even more fearful of acknowledging free choice, and so end up denying it even more strongly.

What I'm suggesting is something else completely: that the difference is in whether or not you genuinely believe you've got real, open, free choices about what and how much you eat. The difference is in your attitude. *It has nothing at all to do with what and how much you are eating.* It's entirely possible not to eat for long periods of time and not feel deprived. It's entirely possible to feel tempted by food but not eat it and still not feel at all deprived.

The reason is because you're remembering that it's your own free choice; that nothing about this is being done to you against your will.

This will take some effort on your part. This isn't an instant, magic cure, but even starting to work with this will produce some results, and hopefully this will encourage you enough to want to continue. For most people, though, it does take a while to become real, and more than just an idea you read about in a book.

Consider this, though. It could be that this is the only way you can ever develop control over your eating. This might be it! Perhaps there never will be a pill you can take, a magic formula or a saviour who will come along and sort out this problem for you. It could be that you either continue to think in ways that make this problem worse, however gradually, over the years of your life. Or, you start to make changes, however gradually, that lead to you living more as you want to: in control of what you eat, healthier and enjoying a stronger sense of self-esteem that enhances everything in your life.

The key will be to experience what a difference it

makes in your relationship with food when you think in terms of having choices. And you can only do that when you acknowledge your freedom to eat anything and everything you can get your hands on. When you make that connection, that experience will be of great significance to you because you will know it puts everything into a completely different context.

It works better if you have good reasons for the choices you are making. In other words, you know what is motivating you, what is at stake. If you are clear about your motivation, you'll be able to make choices that you won't regret later on. That's what we'll look at in our next chapter.

WHAT YOU CAN DO

▸ Remind yourself you have completely free choices whenever you think about eating. Tell yourself, 'I can continue to eat like this' or 'I don't ever have to stop overeating' whenever you eat anything. It can take some repetition to get it to sink in and become a reality for you.

It's especially important to do this if you are eating in a compulsive way and feeling out of control. This when you are most likely to revert to prohibitive thinking, so it's crucial to counteract this and reconnect with a strong sense of choice. This means recognising that you can go on bingeing, that you can overeat all your life and that you never have to stop. You've got these choices – whether you want them or not and whether you act on them or not.

▸ Whenever you're in a restaurant or food shop, let yourself know you can eat anything you want, as much as you want. And you can return the next day and eat even more. Then, you freely choose what works for you.

▸ Make complete choices by acknowledging the outcome you would expect, based on your experience. For example, 'I'm choosing to eat this tub of ice cream and to feel nauseous and guilty afterwards'. You are free to eat anything, but different choices produce different outcomes. What you don't have much of a choice about is what outcomes follow from particular choices.

▸ If you feel deprived whenever you don't eat something you fancy, it's because you haven't yet created a good sense of choice for yourself. You might be paying lip service to the idea, you might understand the theory of it, but you don't yet feel it and experience it as a reality. That's OK! This is where many people start. The challenge for you is to continue to reinforce this theme of choice, so that eventually it becomes real.

▸ If you detect a rebellious quality to your eating, the same thing applies. Rebellion is only possible when there's a rule or restriction in place. It's impossible to rebel if you have complete freedom, so remove the sense of prohibition and all the rebelliousness evaporates.

▸ Discussing these ideas as little as possible with the people in your life can give you a better sense of your own choices. It's your own thinking you want to focus on. No matter what anybody else says, it's your own thinking that makes all the difference.

▸ When you ask yourself, 'Am I choosing?' see if you feel and believe you are totally free to overeat - especially when you're not eating something that looks good.

MIRIAM'S STORY

I'm a mother of three, a wife and a manager of a software company. I did Gillian's seminar about a year ago and my eating has transformed, I would say. I do slide occasionally but I have many very good weeks now.

I think the major thing that still grabs me is this thing about choice. I simply refused to put myself back in prison by stopping dieting. But, I'm eating a lot fewer biscuits, for example. I know now that it's my free choice; that I can do it if I want to but I don't have to. I used to eat so much simply because I thought I wouldn't be able to later on, so I wanted to get as much in while I still could.

It was like I was always on the verge of a famine. I was completely caught up in the trap of repeatedly dieting and bingeing, dieting and bingeing, for several years. I would go to various kinds of slimming groups and be eating frantically as soon as I had been weighed. I used to have this thing about Sundays, because I would always start my diet again on Monday and I used to eat all day Sunday. Today it's Sunday and I'm just delighted about the way I have eaten. I was thinking earlier I'd have some toast, and I thought no, I'll wait for supper. It seems so normal to think that way now and yet it was never like that before. There was always so much of a struggle.

It's had an effect on other things in my life as well. I'm more conscious when I say I've 'got to' do something. I didn't get it at first, but I now realise the things I take on are my choice, and then it isn't a burden. In general I like being busy but often it gets too much.

The benefit to me is definitely in terms of self-esteem and it's a huge relief not to be on that diet bandwagon. I really enjoy eating and I really enjoy feeling in control. I feel liberated. I'm going to make a cabbage salad this evening. I positively enjoy that sort of thing now.

CHAPTER TWO
WHY DOES IT MATTER TO ME?

Why are you reading about an alternative to dieting? The chances are it's because you want to lose weight. Everywhere you look – at your friends, at TV, in magazines – people are talking about wanting to lose weight. They say things like:

'I'm tired of living in this fat body.'
'I look in the mirror and I'm depressed for the rest of the day.'
'If only I was thinner my life would be so much better.'
'I'd love to walk into a room and not feel self-conscious because of my size.'
'I've struggled with my weight all my life.'
'If I could win the lottery or be thin, I'd rather be thin.'

Of course there's no shortage of solutions offered to help you lose weight. Diets, low-fat foods and slimming clubs all promise to take inches off your thighs and fat off your backside. The problem is *weight* and the solution is to *lose it*.

It seems so simple and yet, as we all know, very few people are actually succeeding. The pressure to be slim comes from every angle, yet we are getting heavier and heavier. That should be our first clue that something is wrong. Maybe motivation to lose weight isn't as straight-forward as it seems.

Why don't we try thinking about all this in a completely different way? I'm going to suggest a change in attitude by first of all making an analogy.

Let's imagine that one day you walk into your kitchen and see to your horror that your kitchen floor is flooded with water, three or four inches deep. Now that's a problem for you, isn't it? You panic, grab a mop and bucket and try to get rid of the water, thinking, 'Oh no, all this dreadful water all over the place, how can I make it go away, it's so horrible and wet, and there's so much of it.' And you mop and mop and mop.

In the middle of all this, someone walks in and points out to you that over at the sink the tap is running, the sink is blocked and the water keeps pouring out. You can see what they're saying, but you don't care very much about the tap and the sink. What you really care about is your floor, so that's what you concentrate on, mopping up the floor and fretting about the water. You have some people coming round and you're afraid they'll see the floor and all the dreadful water. You can hide the tap and the sink behind a screen and they'll never know it's there, but they'll be disgusted if all that water is there on the floor. If only you could get the water cleaned up.

You worry about the water for a long time. Whenever you talk about this problem with your friends, you talk about the water on the floor. Whenever your friends talk to you about it, they ask about the water, how deep it is and how you are doing with the mopping. Weeks go by. Then months. Then years. The water is still there, getting deeper and deeper, and you get more and more worried about it as time goes on.

This story illustrates what happens when you focus on the effect of a problem, the water on the floor, instead of its cause, the running tap. The story may seem rather unrealistic, but the chances are that you too have spent most of your time wanting to change the *effect* of your problem instead of the *cause*.

You may have tried to 'mop up' your excess weight by dieting. You may have set weight loss goals for yourself, such as, 'I want to lose a dress size before my summer holidays.' And you've seen success or failure by how much weight you lost or gained. In the analogy, you are chiefly concerned with the floor, gauging success by how dry or wet it is. You know there's a tap running somewhere, but it's not nearly as important, is it?

Clearly there's something here that we all know: in general, dealing directly with the cause of a problem is going to work much better than trying to take care of the effects. In the analogy, if you dealt with the cause by getting the tap and the sink to do the work they were designed for, in time the water would evaporate and it will be fairly easy to keep dry. In the same way, when you eat the food that your body was designed for, in time, the weight evaporates and the weight loss is fairly easy to maintain.

Do you think you've been trying to do this already? Maybe, but it's also likely that your weight has been all that matters. Glance back to the beginning of this chapter and see if you don't identify with those first statements. Isn't that what's motivating you? Weight loss?

Wanting to lose weight is very likely to be the reason you're reading this book. Assuming you are overweight, that's a good reason, but no matter how much you want it, it is a weak motivation. It's weak because it keeps you locked into the effect of the problem. You're just trying to mop up the water. Endlessly. This is an important reason why so few people are succeeding, even though they want it so much.

Now when you think about it, dealing with the cause of a problem is the obvious answer, so, you might ask, why doesn't everybody just figure this out for themselves? There are a number of reasons for this, but perhaps the most common factor is lower self-esteem. Low self-esteem can keep you locked into seeing your problem *entirely* in terms of the size and the shape of your body. Low self-esteem means that making the switch from effect to cause, far from being obvious and simple, is in fact a challenge. This will help you towards motivating yourself in a much more powerful way, so let's understand it a bit.

Low self-esteem often means that being slimmer – improving your appearance – is all that matters. Very crudely put, it's like thinking something like this: 'I don't think very much of myself, but if I looked really good or at least better than I do now, I might convince people that I'm OK and maybe worth having around.'

This creates a dreadful relationship with food. One extreme example is someone who eats a chocolate bar for lunch, a packet of crisps for dinner and wouldn't dream of sitting down to a real meal because it has too many calories in it. Such a person places so little value on herself or himself they don't regard their health as worth supporting.

That's extreme, but it could be that you too make many decisions about what you eat based on what you look like rather than your nutritional needs. This way of thinking about food is, at least in large part, based on the judgment of others. It reinforces the low self-esteem, which in turn reinforces this way of thinking.

You might think, as many do, that if only you lost weight, your self-esteem would improve because you'd feel so proud of yourself. But it doesn't work that way, as many people who have achieved their ideal weight know too well. I've often heard people say they felt as bad about themselves when they were skinny as when they were fat. Often that surprised them because they thought that 'looking good' would solve everything.

Sometimes, though, you hear people say, 'Yes, losing weight is wonderful but it's not the most important thing, because I really enjoy so much about the way I'm living now.' That's much closer to what I'm getting to, and I want to suggest that the people who think like this tend to be more successful in the long term. What made all the difference is they found ways to motivate themselves to eat less that aren't *exclusively* about how much they weigh and what they look like.

Don't get me wrong; it's a very good idea to lose weight, assuming of course that you are overweight to start with. It's when you can put that to one side and discover other reasons to take control of your overeating that things really start to change. You lose weight too, but it's a side effect rather than the focus of everything. Then, your weight loss is much more likely to last. (9)

There are a number of reasons why weight loss doesn't work – both short and long term - as your main motivation. First of all, it gives you delayed feedback. For example, if you didn't eat some rubbishy snacks after dinner one evening, you could wake up the next morning feeling more alert and energised. That's far more rapid feedback, letting you know you're on the right track, than the tiny bit of weight you *might* have lost. It's also much more clearly connected to that particular choice you made about not overeating the previous evening. It's not so easy to say that any one binge will end up as any one particular bulge of fat on your hips!

Most important of all, though, is that motivating yourself to lose weight only works until your weight is lost. When you've lost weight, there's no longer any good reason not to overeat – and so you do! So, pay attention to all the other things that are at stake, such as feeling in control, having more energy, no stomach aches or headaches, sleeping better, clearer thinking or more positive mood.

It's these sorts of things that can motivate you – if you notice and pay attention to them – even before you've lost very much weight. This is especially important if you have a lot of weight to lose. As you may know, it's a slow process, and losing two pounds after a week, although a brilliant result, can seem a drop in the ocean. So, look for anything else that you might be enjoying because you've been eating less. Make a point to remember these things, as they will continue to provide you with motivation, greatly reducing the likelihood that you will yo-yo back up again.

This is a different way to motivate yourself and it's a way that's much more effective, especially over the course of a lifetime. (10)

It's about eating in a way that supports and enhances your emotional and your physical wellbeing. It's about correcting the balance from a situation where losing weight is everything to just having it be one factor. It's fine to have both kinds of motivation. Most of us do. We will always want to look as good as we can, and I do too. What makes the difference in achieving this is having both of these kinds of motivation in a good balance.

When you draw the focus of your attention away from your weight and towards looking after your health, you immediately start to boost your self-esteem. This is because you are affirming that you value yourself enough to give your body what's best for it.

You motivate yourself towards having a healthy relationship with food rather than looking a certain way. You can have both. You can have the best of health and look great too, but when you prioritize your health and self-esteem you will connect with a considerably more powerful and enduring source of motivation. Then, the weight loss pretty much takes care of itself.

WHAT YOU CAN DO

▸ Identify any motivation you may have that's not about weight loss. It's not that losing weight is a bad thing; it's just that we need to correct an imbalance, because weight loss – what other people see and judge us by – has become much too important in most people's minds. Is there anything you like about eating less, besides losing weight? Make the effort to notice how your life is better when you eat in healthier ways. Do you have more energy to get through your day, so that you enjoy your evenings more? Fewer headaches? Better digestion? Do you notice that your self-esteem is higher? Is it simply that you enjoy being in control of your eating, that you feel at peace with yourself?

▸ It will help you to write these things down to make sure you remember them later on. Write as much as you can, with your own personal details. And leave out anything to do with your size, shape and weight. It might take a bit of thinking about this before you can come up with complete answers, but every time you do you'll be developing much better motivation.

▸ Take note of any signs of poor (or just not-so-great) health you may have. You could think of them as messages sent from your body asking you to make changes in what and how much you eat. Many people these days are eating in ways that upset various processes in the body, and then take medication to suppress the symptoms of that upset, instead of changing what they eat. Not such a good idea.

▸ If appearance is your primary motivation, find ways to play it down so that you can create a more sustainable perspective. Instead of setting weight loss targets, aim to eat in a way that best supports your physical and emotional wellbeing. Whenever you think about your weight, remind yourself of those other benefits.

This probably won't come naturally at first; it takes deliberate effort. Discuss your weight as little as possible, whether you've lost some or not, and refuse to join conversations about dieting and weight. If someone says something like, 'You look good – have you lost weight?' say as little about it as possible and then change the subject if you can.

▸ Be especially careful any time you lose weight. Have you ever lost weight and immediately started eating more? It's very common. Losing weight gets you attached to that effect again, taking you off track with the cause. This is one place you can see just how counterproductive weight loss is as motivation. Especially at first, keep as quiet as you can about any lost weight, concealing it under baggy clothes and not mentioning it to anyone. Sounds crazy, doesn't it? But it works.

It's best to think of weight loss as being a kind of anti-motivation that gets in the way of more effective motivation, which is your health and self-esteem. It makes a big difference because then you move from motivation that reinforces lower self-esteem towards motivation that reinforces higher self-esteem. And it's higher self-esteem that will continue to work for you in the longer term.

▸ If you want to lose weight for your health, don't assume this chapter has no relevance. Many people are aware of the health risks of their excess weight and still have a strong emotional attachment bound up in their appearance. Also, at least to a very large extent, it's the change in *eating* that improves your health.

▸ Find ways to improve the quality of your meals. Are you one of those people who have settled for a mediocre way of eating, telling yourself it's healthy when in fact it could be quite a bit better? Are you still counting calories? Start to think in terms of eating for nutritional needs. Counting calories means you're focused on weight loss. Caring more about the nutritional content of your meals means you are building your health and self-esteem. More about this later.

▸ When you ask yourself, 'Why does it matter to me?' find any reason that doesn't depend on losing weight. When you consider eating something, ask yourself how you expect you'll feel after you've finished. Guilty, bloated and lethargic? Or energized, liberated and at peace with yourself? That's how you make your choices.

It's important to use your own experiences. My main motivation is to slow down the process of aging, to stay younger and healthier for longer in my life. But sometimes I might not have a snack because I know I'll enjoy my next meal more. It can be just that simple. You strengthen your self-esteem in the here and now when you motivate yourself in these ways. Weight loss will follow – and it is much more likely to last.

MARTHA'S STORY

Self-esteem is what clicked for me. I've been through a lot of traumas recently and I've been very low and this has been a way forward for me. At the moment I'm clearing all the junk out of my house, throwing it all out, and that's all been part of it. So it's been a whole life change.

I know it's not about weight but I've lost 14 pounds so far. I'm not completely happy with my eating but I'm not bingeing any more so that's nice. I'd like to find better ways to cook vegetables and plan my menus ahead of time and I'm not doing that yet. I'm making things up as I go along and too often that degenerates into lots of ready-made meals and sandwiches. So that's one of the things I still want to change.

The changes have been gradual and sensible and it's definitely lasting. I don't fear that suddenly I'm going to start bingeing again, day after day, like I used to. I may overeat once but it's not the end of the world. I know it won't mean going down that slippery slope into that scary out of control stuff. Overeating is just not OK with me.

This new perspective on things has helped me sharpen up my eating so much. It's about honouring myself and the impact that has on everything and every aspect of your life. I feel so much better now, when I think about all of it I just feel good.

I joined a gym and started exercising but I found it so boring I didn't keep it up. Now I take the dog for a walk every day. A long walk, for about an hour, and I prefer that. I get up in the morning and take the dog out before I go to work.

Sometimes in the evenings I can walk for hours.

I'm thinking about choices a lot more and I'm much more likely to think, 'Do I really have to do this?' And often I don't. This doesn't mean I'm doing less. I'm feeling even more productive these days, and creative and on top of things in general. I'm doing things because I want to do them, not because I have to.

CHAPTER THREE
HOW AM I DEALING WITH TEMPTATION?

You might call it an impulse or an urge. You might call it a snack attack. You fancy something. You want to eat when you know you're not hungry. You want to go on eating when you've just finished a meal. It's happening in all those moments when you wish you had some control. Many people call it a craving. For reasons we'll look at in a moment, it's what I call an 'addictive desire to eat'. (11)

The chances are you think of your desire to overeat as an enemy because it seems to make you eat despite your very best intentions. It seems to overpower you, or sneak up on you when you're not paying attention, so the only way you can think of to escape its power is to avoid it. So, if being bored brings it on you try to keep busy. If eating out holds the most temptation for you, you stop going to restaurants. If you tend to overeat in front of the TV, you turn it off and find other ways to fill your evenings.

Eventually, though, your addictive desire returns. You try to satisfy it with a glass of water or a carrot stick, but what you really want is something much more sugary and creamy. Or you find you really can stop eating all the rubbish food but you overeat healthy food instead. So you continue to satisfy your addictive desire to eat, and wonder how you will ever be able to stop eating so much.

Most people know that running away from a problem does nothing to solve it. Yet this is the very strategy they try to use to control their overeating. At first it might seem to work, but only up to a point, and the reason it stops working is simply that it's impossible to avoid temptation forever. Food is there in your life every day, almost everywhere you go, and a lot of it will tempt you. As if you didn't know that already!

So let's look at an alternative, because there really is another way of approaching this, a way that's different to anything you've ever tried before. It's such an unconventional solution, though; this way may at first seem very strange, impossible and even outrageous. It may take a while before you can really grasp it – but when you do you'll find it works like a charm.

What I'm going to suggest is that you look at this addictive desire to eat and think of it as your friend instead of your enemy. Well, I did say outrageous, didn't I? Bear with me, just continue to read and see if there aren't some things here that give you a glimpse that this may be, not only possible, but extraordinarily effective.

Just consider that if you did make friends with your desire to overeat, you wouldn't fear it and you wouldn't need to run away from it. But most of all, you wouldn't have to satisfy it. You'd feel genuinely tempted from time to time and you'd feel absolutely fine about that. Maybe sometimes you'd eat in response to that temptation, *but you wouldn't have to*. In this way you'd be able to keep yourself from eating so much, not because you'd avoided temptation but because you'd learned to live with it, happily and easily. The best thing about all this is that by taking this approach, your addictive desire diminishes both in intensity and frequency.

There are good reasons why I don't call it a craving. A craving is a more intense and miserable experience, and you know from Chapter One that this is created by the state of deprivation. Cravings are part of the temper tantrum of the deprived child who wants something they can't have. When you create a feeling of free choice for yourself – and this may need to be recreated from time to time as you remind yourself that you've got choices – those more intense, persistent and less acceptable cravings will evaporate.

Not only that, but the word 'craving' doesn't necessarily describe this experience of desire. An addictive desire to eat can be strong at times, especially when you're first working with this approach – but it can also be extremely subtle.

Sometimes it's no more than a brief thought: 'Oh yes, I'd like some of that'. Or it might just appear as your preference for a higher carbohydrate option. This is not what we usually think of as craving, so I use the term 'addictive desire' to include stronger feelings, fleeting thoughts and food preferences. (12)

It's important to be able to identify even those brief thoughts of desire because a great deal of overeating can get done in a fairly unconscious way. You may not be aware you are feeding an addictive desire, and maybe not too aware of what and how much you're eating either. It's impossible to control something you aren't aware of, so noticing your desire to eat is a crucial first step. If you just think in terms of 'craving' you might miss a lot of it.

Becoming aware of addictive desire is, of course, just the first step. It's a hugely significant step, but even when you've identified it, you're still feeling a desire to overeat. When you learn how to manage this experience, you've got the option not to satisfy your desire, or at least not to satisfy it quite so often. This is where we get back to that idea of making the desire your friend.

As with any friendship, understanding goes a long way. Essentially, your addictive desire to eat is your expectation of eating. The term 'addictive' means it's not a genuine need for food, either in terms of quantity (far too much) or in terms of quality (stuff you don't need). The best way to understand it is as a memory; it's the memory you have of overeating in the past.

It's easy to check this out in your own experience. If you have a snack every time you walk into your kitchen, then walking into your kitchen will make you want a snack. If you eat every time you feel upset, then every time you feel upset you'll want to eat something. If you buy a chocolate bar every time you pay for petrol when you fill your car, you will inevitably desire your treat every time you're there. (13)

This is called the 'conditioned response' and was first described by the scientist Ivan Pavlov. He rang a bell every time he fed his dogs and then observed that the dogs salivated any time they heard the bell, thinking food was on its way. In the same way, we train ourselves to associate food with all kinds of cues in our lives. And, as with the dogs, the response can be physical; not only salivation but also what feels like stomach hunger and genuine need.

This is why your addictive desire to eat can at times be felt as sensations in your body. Body and mind are powerfully connected, in two-way communication all the time, so thoughts often show up as physical feelings. For example, the thought, 'Oh no I've locked my keys in the car!' can produce an undeniable sinking feeling the stomach. In the same way, the thought of wanting to eat can show up as a sensation of hungry emptiness.

Well, maybe it is hunger, I hear you say. Not if you've just finished a meal it isn't. That's your addictive desire to eat: you thinking you want more simply because that's what you've done in the past. It's your addictive desire, and it wants to be satisfied.

This is why you can sometimes eat and eat and eat and eat and eat and not satisfy this addictive appetite until you become really uncomfortable and upset with yourself. You reach a state of aversion, which turns off the addictive desire, so then you stop eating.

The addictive desire isn't just any ordinary memory, though. It's produced by a burst of dopamine in the brain, reminding us that eating is pleasurable. It's pleasurable because we are rewarded with endogenous opioids when we eat, because our survival system assumes we're doing something that will keep us alive. Food that contains sugar, most other carbohydrates such as wheat, and fat activate these rewards much more powerfully, which is what makes them more attractive – and potentially more addictive. (14)

This is why you experience a feeling of *desire* for them, rather than an impartial memory of having eaten them in the past. Even when you eat healthy food you'll feel rewarded with pleasure and satisfaction, and that's why eating anything at all can awaken a desire for more.

Understanding that your addictive desire is an inevitable memory helps you to accept that it is a part of your life. It doesn't mean you are mad, bad or greedy. It doesn't mean you're doing anything wrong and that you need to do something – go into therapy or eat exactly the right things – to make it go away. It simply means you've eaten something in this circumstance in the past and you have a memory of that. You've got many choices, but one choice you don't have is to instantaneously erase your memory.

You either reinforce this memory by overeating once again, or you start to let it go by leaving it unsatisfied. If you leave the addictive desire unsatisfied, you get to be in control of your overeating, and it fades because you are no longer feeding and reinforcing it. More on this later.

You may be thinking that it's going to be tough to make friends with something that seems to overwhelm and control you. You may know that the addictive desire can put you into a kind of trance, when you want to eat, and all other thoughts disappear from your mind. You forget why you wanted to stop eating so much. You forget how good you feel when you eat more wisely. You get mesmerised and all you can think about is food.

When, in the past, you avoided temptation and any feeling of desire, you never learned how to work through this trance state, so you are going to be controlled by it when it's there. Far more powerful is to develop the skill of talking yourself through it, by turning around to face it and deal with it. At first, though, even when you do face it, you may still fight it and struggle with it, simply because you hate it and really you just wish it would go away. This actually makes things worse because the more you fight something like this the more it is going to fight back. (15)

You stop fighting your addictive desire by accepting it, so that, without any opposition, it simply flows through you. You let yourself relax, breathe into the feeling and allow your addictive desire to eat be there.

This doesn't mean that you're enjoying yourself; it is, after all, an uncomfortable sensation of feeling unsatisfied. However, ask yourself if you are willing to feel uncomfortable for a while. In doing so, you learn how to think yourself out of and break the trance by paying attention to the sensation and choosing to let yourself experience it.

Accept it by standing back from it and observing it. Know that it's not you, but a conditioned memory you've developed, or perhaps were encouraged to develop when you were too young to know any better. This standing back from it can be seen in the difference between, 'I'd love an ice cream' and 'This is an addictive desire for ice cream.'

Accepting it makes things a lot easier. It's best to accept it unconditionally, but mostly you'll find that if you really are choosing to accept it, it doesn't hang around for nearly as long. There may be times, especially at first, when it's there a lot, but this does diminish. Paradoxically, the more you genuinely accept it, the more it fades.

Accept it by thinking of this uncomfortable, unsatisfied desire as the price you pay for the control over food that you want. If someone offered you a fortune to accept feeling your addictive desire just once, I wouldn't be surprised if you'd do it. So, it's just a matter of figuring out for yourself whether what you're really going to get is worth it to you. What you get isn't a fortune in money, but the good fortune of the quality of your life and your health when you are eating less. That is exactly how you take control of overeating, by re-evaluating your priorities. *You can only do that – properly – while you are feeling your unsatisfied addictive desire to eat.*

It's not possible to learn how to swim without being in some water. It's not possible to learn how to drive without getting into a vehicle. In the same way, you will not learn how to free yourself from overeating until you let yourself experience your unsatisfied addictive desire to eat and talk yourself through it.

I find this concept is often quite difficult for people to really understand, but makes the biggest difference when they do. Often people will make all kinds of sincere plans about how they are going to eat more sensibly, but they forget about their addictive desire. Then, when temptation strikes, their plans are forgotten and they are left wondering why they didn't follow through.

It's fine to want to make changes, to have an intention, for example, to eat less bread. Just remember that this choice doesn't actually get made until it's 10.30 and you're thinking about fixing your mid-morning, toasty snack. It's how you deal with that experience of desire at that moment in time that makes all the difference.

Of course it's crucial to know you've got free choices about what you do, but often people think in terms of making a choice 'to eat' or 'not to eat' something. So they think, 'Shall I eat the toast or not?' That is the result, but it's not the best way to think about it. It's much better to put powerful words to the process because by describing it correctly you create an entirely new attitude.

The best way is to think, 'Right now, I've got an addictive desire to eat.' Even if that's as far as you go, that will be something, but it's best not to stop there. Then, you can say, 'I could go ahead and satisfy this desire by eating some toast or I could just let myself feel this unsatisfied addictive desire. Yes, it feels uncomfortable but I'd rather have this feeling than spend the rest of my life overeating. It's worth it to me because it means I'll feel more in control and I'll enjoy my lunch more.'

The more you make your choices in this way, the easier it will become and the more natural it will seem. You make the addictive desire your friend because when you accept it you get to break free from overeating and all that goes with it. You let it live with you because by doing so, as a direct result, you can control what and how much you eat.

You accept it because it will change your life. It could even save your life. What you are doing is facing up to the difficulty of making genuine, lasting change in your relationship with food. What you are doing is dealing with this problem in your everyday, practical experience. You choose. The way you choose is either to satisfy your addictive desire or to accept it by being willing to feel it by leaving it unsatisfied. Fundamentally, those are the choices that are open to you and by far the best way to think about them.

Of course you aren't going to stop eating entirely, so one of the challenges you face is knowing the difference between an addictive desire and a genuine need to eat. Contrary to popular belief, we don't possess bodies that can naturally provide us with this information. Our bodies want to get us to eat as much as possible, whenever possible, and even as little as one hundred years ago that really wasn't much of a problem.

These days there's so much food around, and especially so much manufactured, addictive food. Instead of trying to rely on bodies (and brains) that are better suited to another era, we need to think ourselves out of this problem.

So you can get better at identifying your addictive desire, let's look briefly at what it isn't.

NATURAL HUNGER is a sense of emptiness in your stomach, a natural signal from your body telling you it's time to eat. It will come and go, and although it's wise to eat something soon, you won't feel compelled to eat unless it's accompanied by addictive desire. In fact, you can feel perfectly happy, energised and alert when your body isn't being overworked by digesting food all the time.

It's fine to aim for natural hunger at meal times, but don't worry if you don't feel it. For many reasons it can go missing when logic tells you it really should be there, and it could be that you realise how hungry you are only after you've started eating. (16)

Not only is natural hunger unreliable, but waiting until you feel hungry before you eat can be inconvenient, when you need to fit in meal times with other people. It might not be practical to eat later on when you'll be running errands, teaching a class or attending a meeting.

You may in the past have been advised to eat only when you feel hungry, but you can get into difficulty with food because you continually fall short of this impossible goal. This is why it's best to simply consider when it would be appropriate to eat again.

There will always be some guesswork here, but make your best guess about what you think is reasonable, rather than addictive. Every day you'll have opportunities to adjust your guesses, and the better you get at managing your addictive desire, the easier this will become. (17)

ACID INDIGESTION can be so painful that many sufferers overeat to try to keep themselves from feeling it. Antacid medications are not good for your health if you take them long term, so it's much better to correct the problem directly.

As with a lot of illness, there's no one solution that works for everyone, so trial-and-error is the way to go. Excess alcohol and caffeine often contribute to over-acidity, but cigarette smoking can be the biggest cause.

As for food, I had a bad time with acid indigestion until I eliminated wheat and rye. Cutting down on sugar can help a lot, as well as getting regular exercise and plenty of water. Acid indigestion could indicate the development of more serious health problems in time, so it's important to deal with this, quite apart from eliminating this cause of false hunger.

LOW BLOOD SUGAR comes from the rapid rise and fall of insulin and glucose in the bloodstream caused by overeating carbohydrates. This, of course, has been written about for so long by so many people I'm not going to spend a lot of time repeating it here. This can be an important factor for many people, and perhaps become more so as you get older.

If you often feel hungry, irritable or drowsy during the day, especially mid-morning, mid-afternoon or soon after eating, low blood sugar could be the reason. Here is an example that has come up a few times in my seminars. Someone eats what they consider to be a substantial, healthy breakfast of commercial cereal or wheat toast but gets so hungry by mid-morning they have great difficulty waiting until lunch time before they eat again. Eating a larger breakfast doesn't make things any better. Eating low carbohydrate breakfast – just eggs and bacon, for example – makes the crucial difference.

If you experience these sudden and otherwise inexplicable drops of energy, think back to what you last ate and see if it included starchy carbohydrates such as wheat and sugar. Your brain needs a steady supply of glucose to function, so you could feel sluggish mentally as well when your blood glucose falls.

Your biggest breakthrough comes by understanding that your addictive desire to eat is not just something to be endured; it actually makes real change possible. When it's dealt with properly, this excess appetite fades from your life. This is partly because you are no longer reinforcing it by overeating and partly because you are paying attention to this process. We look at how this happens in our next chapter.

WHAT YOU CAN DO

▸ Aim to notice your addictive desire to eat as often as you can, so that you develop the awareness you need. It's only when you've identified it that you can make a choice about it; if you aren't aware of it, it will control you.

‣ Don't be put off by the word 'addiction'; I do not use it to condemn or judge. All it refers to is the food you eat that you don't actually need, and it's always a matter of degree. It could be that you've got just a few addictive eating patterns and don't overeat that much. Even so, thinking in terms of addiction is extremely helpful.

‣ You take control of your overeating by allowing yourself to feel your unsatisfied addictive desire - but don't expect to do that every time. Sometimes you might not even notice the desire, and sometimes you might not be willing to accept it. This is a process, and you will be on a learning curve. Stay with it and you will get where you want to go, but don't ever expect your eating to be perfect from now on.

‣ If at first it's difficult to identify, try setting a time goal so that you can see your addictive desire more clearly. Setting a time goal means you agree with yourself that you intend not to eat until a certain time, perhaps in an hour or two. Do this during those times when you want to take control of snacking and grazing. Remember that you've got the option of eating, even before you get to your chosen time. Aim to observe and manage any desire to eat you may feel up to the time you've selected.

‣ Eating a meal is likely to create your addictive desire for more, which is why meals can seem never to end. Have a clear picture in your mind of what you intend to eat before you start. When you finish this amount (assuming it's less than usual) you'll want to go on eating, and this is your addictive desire. You can practice managing this desire at the end of your meals.

▸ Be willing to end your meals feeling unsatisfied. The advice to 'eat until you're full' doesn't take the addictive desire into account. Most people want to continue eating after finishing a meal of a reasonable size. It's entirely possible that you never feel satisfied until you've overeaten so much you're physically and psychologically uncomfortable, much too full, and even feeling guilty and disappointed with yourself. Your way out of this night-mare is to allow yourself to feel unsatisfied when you end your meal.

▸ Aim to notice when you've fallen into that trance-like state of desire during a meal, and you are eating much too fast. It might not be possible to stop this immedi-ately, but any time you become aware that you are eating too fast, sit back in your chair, put your fork down, take a breath... and then resume eating. In time you will get used to eating more slowly, and with more awareness.

▸ There may be no need to abstain from your 'binge' or 'trigger' foods. Whenever you eat your favourite 'drug', be it sugar, chocolate, nuts, bread or whatever, your addictive desire for them will be awakened. It might be easier for you to cut them out completely, but abstinence can be unrealistic long term, and not at all necessary once you are able to manage addictive desire. It's so important to eat in a way you can continue to live with, to have some flexibility and variation. More on this later.

▸ When your favourite, addictive foods are close at hand, you're likely to feel more of a desire for them just because they are so available. It might be better not to have some things in the house because they drive you crazy, so find what works best for you. At least be aware that by having certain things around you, your addictive desire for them may be more persistent. You might find it works better to accept your addictive desire for them when you're in the supermarket, and choose to leave them there on the shelves.

▸ Notice the difference between an enjoyment of food, which is both positive and appropriate, and the 'high' you get when you satisfy your addictive desire. It's important to enjoy what you eat, but some people eat so much highly addictive food – usually sugars, wheat and fats – they lose their taste for proper food such as vegetables.

Junk food satisfies your addictive desire. Real food satisfies your nutritional needs. They are quite different experiences and it will help you to learn how to tell them apart. This is especially important if you tend to justify overeating by thinking, 'I really enjoy my food – what's wrong with that?'

▸ Remind yourself why you're accepting this unsatisfied desire by thinking of what benefit eating less will bring you. Look for reasons other than weight loss and find your own reasons. It may be energy or it may be a sense of freedom, control or accomplishment. Just have it be something for yourself, something that's a joy to you in your life.

Then it will be easier for you to accept the uncomfortable feeling of unsatisfied desire – because the trade-off is a good one as far as you're concerned.

▸ Intense and persistent cravings are sure signs you're feeling deprived and it's vital you change your way of thinking so that this doesn't wear you down. If you're feeling deprived it's because you don't believe that you've got complete freedom about what you do. You might hold out until a good excuse comes along – but when you feel deprived you might even create a good excuse if one doesn't show up on its own.

▸ Ask yourself, 'How am I dealing with temptation?' and notice your addictive desire and what you're doing about it. Feeding it unconsciously? Or paying attention to it and thinking it through?

You could begin to notice and make choices to accept this desire to eat as the trade-off for the benefits that come from eating less. The more you do that, the less you will be overeating. And in time your addictive desire to eat will fade.

KAREN'S STORY

I had been obese for almost ten years and I had high blood pressure and a strong fear that I would become diabetic. I had talked about this with my doctor and she often warned me about my weight. I had dieted all my life and failed at it all my life. I felt really quite miserable about the whole thing. Nothing I did worked, but it wasn't for lack of trying.

I did a counselling course for years and went through endless hours of counselling in a determined effort to get to the bottom of my overeating. There were other issues too and the counselling helped a lot with some of them, but my eating was always the main problem and the one that felt impossible to change.

I always believed that if I could only find the root cause of my eating problem, find out what was behind it and heal that, then I would be able to stop overeating. This assumption, far from being challenged by the people running the course, was actively encouraged. For much of my life I carried around a strong sense that there was something wrong with me, something I could never discover and which my overeating continuously confirmed.

All that's changed now. When I did Gillian's seminar I kept waiting for the other shoe to drop, waiting for the cravings to return, but they never did. My addictive desire is a completely different thing, nothing like I used to feel when I was dieting, or I should say, trying to diet.

I never before had made the connection between what I ate

and the state of my health. Before, it was always about weight, about how I looked. Now eating healthy foods and not eating unhealthy ones makes tremendous sense. It's all so obvious to me now but you can get yourself into such amazing muddles about food and eating and weight.

The concept that remains with me the most is about the addictive side of eating because I now know what to do when I'm feeling 'hungry' which of course isn't feeling hungry at all. It doesn't happen nearly as much as it used to, it's changed. I'm realising there are periods of time when I have this addictive hunger, and that I don't have to satisfy it.

At the moment I'm doing a 28-day detox and I find it very interesting because I'm not eating wheat. I hadn't realised how very 'more-ish' bread was, and that's something that's really come home to me. I'm eating rye bread on this detox so I'm still eating bread, but I'm not doing that continuous nibbling that I used to do with the regular bread.

CHAPTER FOUR
HOW TO GET A NEW BRAIN

Have you ever thought you'd need a new brain before you could control your overeating? I've heard people say this in my seminars. Well, guess what – you can get one! Not completely new (I expect there are a few bits you'd like to keep) but the part of your brain that makes you want to eat so much can actually be physically altered! By you!

It might sound unbelievable, but this is exactly what will happen when you follow the guidelines set out in this book. It's not really all that bizarre; in fact, it's a natural process that's available to us all. It just helps so much if you understand what it is you're doing, so that you know why you are following a particular course of action. Then you can be more deliberate about it and therefore more effective. So this is what this chapter is about.

First of all, understand a simple principle about how your brain works: that every cell in your brain communicates with other cells. Each cell does this by pulsing signals to the next brain cell, which in turn signals to the next, setting off a chain reaction, one cell to the next, to the next, to the next, hundreds and thousands and millions of times across your brain. It's doing it right now!

There are billions and billions of brain cells, and each signal could travel in any direction. But they don't just scatter at random, the signals tend to go in set networks, and these networks form your familiar ways of thinking.

This is how this happens. When two brain cells have pulsed their signals at the same time on several occasions, they form a relationship so that when one of them now pulses, it's much more likely to make that other one pulse as well. In future they are much more likely to signal together, and this means you get to remember something.

All of your memories and your knowledge are formed by these connections between the cell networks. The more you repeat any thought or action, the more these same cells get activated in the same network and the stronger their connection becomes. *This is especially the case when your brain thinks your survival is at stake, as it does with any food.*

Let's take an example. Let's say, every time you have a particularly tough day at work, you buy some biscuits and ice cream on the way home, and you sit in front of the TV and eat them. You have trained the cells in your brain that think, 'it's been a tough day' to connect to, 'want biscuits and ice cream'. That's the memory you have and the connection you strengthen every time you eat this way after a tough day at work.

The interesting part is how you go about making real changes with this. The key is that when a particular network is no longer reinforced, the cells disconnect. The connections don't disappear instantly but do become weaker and weaker when that particular network of brain cell signaling is no longer reinforced.

So, you might think, why not change your routine and go out to a movie whenever you've had a bad day at work? Won't that weaken the connection? You might know from your own experience that it doesn't.

Avoiding a situation, whatever it is, means avoiding the addictive desire connected with that situation – and you don't change the brain connections this way. I wouldn't be surprised if you've already tried avoiding a situation where you used to overeat, and when you returned to it you also returned to overeating. The reason for this is you never did break that particular connection between that situation and addictive overeating.

In order for the connections to break down, the memory needs to be activated. It's only when that partic-ular network between the cells is active but not reinforced by eating that the connections change and weaken. They don't change merely through the passing of time, or while you're thinking about something else.

This is why you need to experience your memory of

biscuits and ice cream connected to that situation. Perhaps you would notice and manage your desire for them as you pass by the shop where you would have bought them, and again when you're sitting in front of the TV thinking about your lousy day. It's your conscious awareness of the process that makes the crucial differ-ence. What actually works is to pay attention to your experience of addictive desire, because in doing so you actively participate in re-routing the brain signals.

This isn't nearly as difficult or complicated as it may sound. Remember this is happening in our brains anyway. New connections are created in our brains whenever we learn and remember anything, and connec-tions are weakened as we move on in our lives and let go of things that once were hugely significant to us.

A number of psychological issues are treated, successfully, in a very similar way; for example, phobia. This is not to say you have a phobia, just that the process of recovery is similar. People can develop a phobia of almost anything, feeling overwhelmed and even paral-ysed with fear. This condition is treated through exposure to the feared object; a bird, for example. The therapist might show their client a drawing of a bird, a photograph and then perhaps a stuffed bird.

Each of those stages will generate fear, and as they allow themselves to feel and accept this fear it begins to fade. In time, they can be close to birds and even touch and feed them. This is because the brain networks that connected 'birds' to 'fear' have weakened, and their phobia is overcome. This is the principle behind the standard therapy for phobia. The point is that this change doesn't happen without exposure to birds and the experience of fear that initially arises as a result.

In a very similar way, you can expose yourself to your feelings of addictive desire when they occur. When you're feeling your addictive desire to eat, when you want to eat more and you feel unsatisfied, those are the moments when real transformation takes place. This is because you are physically changing the connections in your brain. Research has demonstrated in a controlled, laboratory setting, that a craving for chocolate diminishes - in a way that lasts – when it is experienced but not satisfied. (18)

I'm sure you don't need me to tell you there are a great many connections in our brains associated with wanting to eat. If it was just a bad day at work, that would be one thing, but we integrate addictive eating into our lives, so there are many things that can trigger connections with food. You can breathe a sigh of relief here, because you won't need to face every single one of these connections in order to weaken them all. You'll work on some and others will seem to take care of themselves. However, there will still be many circumstances you'll meet for the first time, which will trigger a real feeling of addictive desire.

For example, let's say you tend to eat whenever you

feel bored. You have established a connection in your brain between feeling bored and eating, so even though you might not feel bored for quite a while, when you do, you'll want to eat.

You break this association when you feel bored and you experience and manage your addictive desire. Those are the moments when you physically rewire that connection between 'I'm bored' and 'I want to eat'. It's not possible to do that if you're not feeling bored and wanting to eat. Then, that connection begins to fade. It might not go completely for ever, but it will be considerably less compelling.

Then there are other connections, say, between overeating and wanting to relax. And wanting to celebrate. And feeling sad. And visiting the local coffee shop (the one where they have those pastries). And taking a break at your place of work. And going to the cinema. Etc. Etc. Sometimes you get an addictive desire to eat for no other reason than something just became available. You caught sight of some food, smelled it or simply knew it was there, and now you want to eat it.

All you need to do about this is to continue to live your life as you normally do, and using the themes outlined in Chapters One, Two and Three, you develop the habit of noticing and making choices about your addictive desire to eat. It's not essential to identify the cue that triggered it; sometimes it's obvious and sometimes it isn't. It can be a subtle thought such as,

'What shall I do now? Oh, I think I'll eat something'. Addictive desire can be triggered by fleeting thoughts and feelings; the slightest annoyance about something or a vague sense of restlessness.

You don't need to replace the overeating with anything; in fact, it works better if you don't, especially at first. It's not like you're going to get a big hole in your brain where your addictive desire to eat used to be! You simply choose to allow yourself to feel these inevitable moments of unsatisfied desire, and so you weaken them, and so they fade. (19, 20)

Knowing this can be so helpful because it's very common for people to make lots of good changes in their eating, take control and do very well for a period of time. Then, perhaps weeks or months later, they encounter a particular circumstance for the first time and they fall back into overeating again. The last time they were in this situation they overate, so there's suddenly a stronger connection, an addictive desire that has yet to fade.

As an example, someone I know, Mary, lives with her family and rarely spends time alone. One day, her family was away visiting a relative while she stayed at home to get some work done. At the end of the day she did a fair bit of addictive overeating. Mary explained it to herself as comfort eating, but another way to explain it is that she had an addictive desire connected to a situation she hadn't come across for a long time. She used to overeat quite a lot when she was single, many years ago.

It's not that her feelings about spending one evening on her own were so unbearable. In fact, she said she enjoyed having some time to herself. It's just that this situation triggered her memory, her addictive desire. Had she accepted this desire and not fed it, it too would have faded in time, even when she was on her own.

Unfortunately, it usually gets satisfied and reinforced, and what also gets reinforced is the sense of utter power-lessness to control eating in certain circumstances. So people say, 'I was doing fine until I went on holiday' or 'until I got stressed at work' or 'until I broke up with my boyfriend' or 'until I stayed at home all day with the kids'. Just remember that all of these present nothing other than more brain connections to be redesigned. As you go through these experiences in your life and no longer reinforce their connections with overeating, they begin to break down. And you don't need to do them all at once.

There's something else about how our brains work that's very helpful to know. To put this as simply as possible, when your addictive desire to eat is triggered, this desire comes from the middle of your brain, roughly in between your ears. This is a more primitive area, one that deals with basic survival needs. If you have ever felt consumed with desire, overwhelmed by it and driven mad with it, this midbrain area was dominating your thinking. You could feel like you really will die if you don't binge on biscuits and ice cream, and there's absolutely no reasoning with it.

In order to bring a more sane perspective to this more intense desire, another part of the brain needs to be brought into play, and this is right at the front of your brain, just behind your forehead. Called the prefrontal cortex (PFC), this is the most adaptable part of your brain and it's the part that's considered the most human. It has been very well established that low activity in this area is strongly related to difficulty with all addictive behaviours. (21)

The PFC enables you to make more of the decisions you won't later regret. It enables you to think twice about what you're going to do. What is most helpful, however, is that the more you can activate it, *the more it calms down the intensity of that stronger craving arising from the midbrain*. (22)

There's a huge amount of research on this subject using brain-scanning technology. Success in taking control of addictive behaviours of all kinds – from crystal meth to food – has been shown to be directly related to the degree of activation in the PFC. (23, 24)

When the PFC becomes extremely damaged through serious injury, people can lose control of any impulse they may have. This kind of injury compels people to follow through on any whim that flips through their mind, and with impulses ruling absolutely, life is chaotic and relationships impossible. This is because they have no ability to reason with themselves, no ability to have any consideration at all that some actions might not be the most wise. (25)

But doctors have found that even physical damage to the brain can be repaired. This is carried out, not through surgery or drugs, but through the brain rebuilding itself. Doctors who specialise in brain rehabilitation, after accidents or strokes for example, have found two things are required: *paying attention* and *repetition*. So, the more you consciously manage your experience of addictive desire, the more you activate and strengthen this frontal area of your brain.

Inasmuch as you have difficulty with food, you have trained yourself not to control one particular kind of impulse, the impulse to overeat. This training may have continued for years and may even have begun in childhood before you had any idea what was happening. It wasn't an injury that impaired this particular brain function, but the effects are similar because you're not using the PFC during moments of desire, just as if it was physically disabled.

In the first part of this chapter we looked at breaking down networks of cell communication, and in a similar way it's important to build and strengthen connections with the PFC. As before, this requires your deliberate repetition *while the addictive desire is happening*.

There are three main concepts to bring to mind that will support activation of your PFC. You will recognise them from our previous chapters:

1. Declare your own freedom of choice in the matter by remembering, 'I'm free to eat anything I can get my hands on, any time.' If you don't assert this to yourself you are likely to assume a prohibitive, diet mentality by default. Research has shown that people don't use the PFC when they are following instructions or established routines. (26)

2. Choose the outcome you'll create by considering how you expect to feel after you've finished overeating. You activate your PFC when you think beyond the immediate pleasure of eating and include the outcome as well. This is where you can recall that list you started making after reading Chapter Two. (27)

3. Use words in your mind to name what's happening: 'this is an addictive desire to eat.' Research shows that observing and putting words to a feeling increases activity in the PFC, thereby lessening the strength of the midbrain. It's deceptively simple, but getting into the habit of noticing and naming your experience as an addictive desire is a huge step forward. (28)

So, when you work with the themes I introduced in Chapters One, Two and Three, you create lasting changes in the way your brain works. Even though it may take huge effort at first to focus on these three themes, every time you do you will be building a capacity to manage and tame the addictive appetite through encouraging activity in your prefrontal cortex.

The aim of this chapter is to help you to understand what's actually happening when you work with this approach. Then, you're not blindly following orders, following directions just because I've told you to. You're using the principles because you understand them, because you know what you're doing.

We have been looking at the ways in which the brain changes, physically, by the ways in which you think – or don't think. This change in brain function doesn't necessarily happen when you follow a diet and it doesn't necessarily happen when you lose weight. And this, essentially, is why the changes you may have made in the past didn't last long term; because your brain had remained the same.

Our brains work in a 'use it or lose it' way, and this is useful to understand for two reasons.

One is to understand that our familiar thoughts become physically etched into our brains, and that's why we tend to get stuck in ruts of habitual behaviour. They really are like ruts or grooves, and it takes some effort to get out of them.

The second thing is that this isn't permanent; these grooves can be changed – probably faster than you realise. You can accept the reality that these familiar networks are there right now, and at the same time begin to make choices to do things differently, knowing that in time and with practice things will get easier. They'll get easier because you'll be getting your brain to work in a different way.

In general, you either strengthen particular connections in your brain or you weaken them – every day, with every encounter with food. Does this sound rather daunting? Well, the best thing about it is that there's room for error. Please don't get the idea that everything rests on the next piece of chocolate you are (or are not?) going to eat!

You may still want to be impulsive around food sometimes, and that's fine. I'm assuming you are way too impulsive around food and you have a tough time controlling that. The odd moments don't matter so much. If you just get better at redesigning these connections, you'll do fine.

WHAT YOU CAN DO

▶ Don't necessarily avoid the situations in which you overeat. They are not problems but opportunities for you to make genuine changes.

In time you may want to develop new routines, such as taking more exercise, but it will be best to do this having first made peace with your addictive desire. Then, when you fall back into your old ways – and who doesn't every now and then? – you won't necessarily fall back into overeating.

‣ You don't need to make all changes at once. See what overeating you really do want to change and be clear about why you want to change it.

‣ Take a couple of deep, slow breaths as you start to work through your addictive desire to eat. This will bring down your level of stress and this, too, improves access to the PFC. Pay attention to the physical sensations associated with the feelings of temptation and desire. The more you actively attend to this process, the better results you get.

‣ The connections between cell networks are stronger when emotions are involved. This is why you may find that your desire to eat is stronger when triggered by feelings such as anger or sadness.

‣ If you substitute another addictive behaviour in the place of eating, such as smoking, drinking or shopping, you will continue to reinforce the same networks, keeping them in business. This is known as 'cross addiction' or 'addiction transfer'. It's not a problem of trading in one addiction for another; it's adding or increasing the strength of another addiction on top of the first one. This is not a good idea, as it doesn't get you anywhere.

‣ However, it's likely there will be times when a substitution is appropriate and not addictive. For example, if you often snack on junk food in the afternoons you might want to eat something healthier instead. Just don't rely on healthy substitutions as the way you deal with your addictive desire, as that will only work up to a point.

▸ Be willing to be repetitive. We all know that repetition is the way we learn, whether learning to write, read, drive or whatever. Even if we just want to remember a phone number or the time of a train we want to catch, we do that by repeating it over and over again.

▸ Be willing to be patient. The patterns in brain activation do change, but not instantaneously. Consider how many years you've been overeating, and don't expect your memory of this to vanish like magic. It's impossible to say how long all this will take, but if you engage in it whole-heartedly we are probably talking about days and weeks rather than months and years.

▸ Connect with these three themes: Do I know I'm free to overeat? What outcomes do I want to create? How am I responding to my addictive desire?

IRIS'S STORY

The seminar raised a lot of awareness and I think the key lesson that remains is awareness of addiction. If you have a situation where you overeat and you remove the overeating from the situation, you create a vacuum. I had always been aware of that but I had never known what to do about it.

Whatever I did; get busy, exercise, socialise, the vacuum was always there. Now for the first time I have a name for it: it's my addictive desire to eat. That's been the big revelation for me, because naming it like that has stripped away all the extra bits and pieces I added to it and attributed to it. It used to mean I was incomplete, immature and somehow different from everybody else. At least, that's what I made it mean but I can easily see now that it's just a memory of something I used to do. That realisation has changed so much for me and continues to do so.

I had been pregnant while I did the seminar and I wanted to do the best for my children and do the best for me. Even though I was enormous, it was because I was carrying twins and not because I had been pigging out!

The seminar reinforced my healthy attitude. Without it I would have used pregnancy as an excuse to overeat, because nobody would know the difference. But I was aware whenever I ate: why was I eating this? I'm more aware of the excuses I would give myself and I realised that pregnancy was a wonderful excuse: 'I'm eating for three!'

CHAPTER FIVE
WHY YOU EAT SO MUCH

It has often been said that when it comes to overeating, it's not *what* you eat, it's *why* you eat that's the key. Why you overeat, for example, is because you're sad, maybe even depressed, and you know that eating something sugary and creamy will comfort you and cheer you up.

Another example might be that you overeat because it brings you pleasure, and after a hard day at work, when you perhaps feel unappreciated, you think you deserve a nice treat of something really yummy to help you to unwind.

This way of thinking is very common, of course, and at first glance may seem to completely explain everything about why you overeat. But there's a problem with it, and this is that most people's experience is that the comfort and pleasure they enjoy from addictive overeating is rather short-lived. It usually lasts, as if I need to tell you, for the time it takes to eat the treat, and sometimes not even that.

For many, their upset about overeating and being overweight is so great that there's little comfort in any eating at all. Even when it's apparent, the comfort and pleasure is often followed by its opposite: some degree of psychological and physical upset, discomfort and regret.

If someone offered to give you some money but in half an hour they would get double the amount back, I imagine you wouldn't be too impressed with the deal. So why do so many people continue to fall for a similar con? We all know that depressed people who eat loads of chocolate every day don't become happier as a result. Stressed people who constantly snack on rubbish don't feel less stressed. Bored people could easily find any number of things to do with their time, other than overeat.

We tell ourselves that overeating is enhancing our life, while at the same time knowing that it is impairing and could even be destroying it. The way to understand why this happens is to understand the addictive desire to eat. When you have an addictive desire, for something sugary for example, that primitive survival system is activated in your brain. Dopamine, released from your mid-brain, takes over your thinking and keeps you focused on getting some food into your mouth.

This survival mechanism got put in place at a time when there wasn't a great deal of food around, and especially no refined sugar or manufactured products.

This survival mechanism is hopelessly out of place in today's food environment, unable to distinguish between your need for cabbage, say, and a box of donuts.

You are being driven by that ancient survival system whenever you feel your addictive desire to eat. Part of that system shows up as thoughts and sensations of desire, and part of it shows up as credible and persuasive reasoning. The dopamine release puts you into an altered state of consciousness, where food is all that matters.

All food activates this reward system to some extent, which is why it's possible to overeat any food at all. However, the starchy carbohydrates such as sugar and wheat, together with fats, activate this survival mechanism more powerfully. Not because they are healthy, but because of the stronger biochemical rewards they activate in your brain. This is why you love them so much and this is why they have the quality of being more addictive. Your ancient brain thinks they are essential for life, when in fact they are the opposite.

Your addictive desire demands to be satisfied, but even though all that activity is going on in your brain, you could be quite unaware of it. For most people, all they are aware of is they keep eating too much - and sometimes they aren't even aware of that!

People don't usually notice that a cue has triggered a burst of dopamine in their brain, so they react automatically, often in a fairly unconscious state. All they may be aware of is how they are explaining their overeating: I'm bored, sad, in need of comfort, stressed, lonely – or whatever.

You explain your overeating, to make sense of what you're doing. But it's not boredom, sadness or stress that causes your overeating. It's because those are the circumstances in which you feel – and satisfy – your addictive desire. It's because those are the circumstances in which dopamine gets released in your brain, insisting that you could die if you don't eat something right now.

Understanding this helps to make a great deal of sense of things. This is why you can overeat when you're depressed but also when you're happy, when you're celebrating and when you're lonely, when you're busy and when you're relaxing. The truth is people overeat in lots of different circumstances. Their explanation simply matches whatever happens to be going on at the time.

This is why examining your feelings, although a fine thing to do, will only produce limited success with eating less. Feeling frustrated and angry about something, for example, could trigger your desire to eat. By all means investigate those feelings and see what you want to do about the frustrating situation. Just know that this doesn't cancel out your addictive desire.

This is why, when we need comforting, it's not enough to take a candle-lit bath, listen to music, spend some time with a loved pet or any of the other things we could do restore our spirits. If feeling comforted were truly our aim, these things would work fine. But none of these things satisfy our addictive desire to eat.

When you begin to notice how you persuade yourself to satisfy your addictive desire to eat, you might see flimsy excuses that no longer make sense to you. But sometimes your reasons can seem rock solid. It could be that you overeat a great deal, not because your addictive desire is so intense and unacceptable, but because you've got some very compelling justifications for satisfying it.

This could be because you're overwhelmed here and now, or because traumatic events happened in your past. The trauma may have passed long ago, but it's remembered, even briefly from time to time, and this becomes a persistent and credible reason to satisfy your addictive desire. You think, 'Bad things happened to me in the past, so I'm going to go ahead and overeat.'

No doubt you call that comfort eating; who wouldn't? You have these bad memories and so you comfort yourself with food. That sounds reasonable, doesn't it? Of course it does, but another way to explain it is that you have an addictive desire to eat, and you habitually justify satisfying it – reinforcing it at the same time – by thinking of these events. You have a free pass to all the eating you ever want to do, and nobody would blame you, including yourself.

It certainly may help you to explore these painful memories, perhaps with the support of a therapist, and gain benefit from that. But if you have already done that and you are still overeating, it's because you haven't yet taken the next step. This is to refuse to use this justification any more and start to make choices to accept your addictive desire instead of satisfying it. You decide that, yes, these dreadful things happened to you, but you don't want to continue to use them to support your overeating.

It's a common idea that those who overeat carry some deep wound that needs to be healed, but that isn't necessarily the way to see it. Sometimes people start to overeat because of some difficulty in their lives, but when the difficulty has passed – and perhaps completely resolved – the addictive relationship with food persists, simply because the addictive desire continues to be fed and reinforced.

In tough times it can seem like a miracle not to overeat, but this could be the one thing in your life you can find delight in at that time. There are a great many things in life that you have no control of and no choice about – but it's wonderful to know that your addictive overeating doesn't have to be one of them! The illusion is that overeating helps you cope with the situation, but the reverse is more likely to be true. Your biggest break-throughs will occur when you discover that difficult emotions don't get any worse when you don't overeat. (29, 30, 31)

If this had happened in the past, it's because you were not managing your addictive desire. When it's not managed effectively, you feel worse because you feel deprived. You get stronger cravings and feel overwhelmed by the sense of self-sacrifice – on top of everything else!

This changes when you take on board that it's always your choice. When you are denying freedom of choice, operating in that state of deprivation, you will attach yourself much more strongly to your justifications. They become crucial because they provide you with the freedom to overeat that you so desperately need. Embracing a real sense of choice means seeing that you can eat whatever you want, and you don't need any excuse at all. Then, those justifications lose their grip.

Remember that when you make your choice, you choose the outcome as well. So if you choose the comfort and pleasure of overeating, also choose what it will cost you: fatigue, perhaps, and feeling out of control. It could also strengthen a sense of victimhood by reinforcing the belief, 'Not only did he/she/it make me feel bad, but they made me overeat as well.' The first step out of this would be to disentangle 'they made me overeat as well' from that scenario. This is a step towards stronger self-esteem and control of overeating.

When you connect with the improved quality of life you get from being in control of your eating, then you can say, 'Either I have this difficult situation in my life and I overeat or I have this difficult situation in my life and I don't overeat.'

And really, what's the difference? The only difference is whether or not the addictive desire is satisfied. Having some control of your eating brings you more confidence and higher self-esteem, and this will support you through tough times far more than overeating ever can. The key here is to be willing to accept, manage and thereby heal the uncomfortable feeling of unsatisfied desire, even when everything else is going badly.

Remember from Chapters Three and Four that your addictive desire to eat will fade when it's managed instead of satisfied. The memory of overeating simply plays itself out until a new memory is formed. When that has happened, you could be in a similar situation and you might not even think about overeating. Then you have the crisis, you have the difficult emotions, and you deal with it all the best you can. You find ways to comfort yourself and restore your sense of optimism about yourself and your life.

It's tough to stay aware of this all the time, so you may miss some of the justifications and overeat. Don't worry if it's just now and again, but if it's happening often, look for the justification you keep using and see how you can let it go. When you're too attached to your justifications too much of the time, it will be tough to manage the feeling of desire without eating.

Doing all this in an imperfect way is something we'll look at in our next chapter.

WHAT YOU CAN DO

▸ It will help you to remember that a justification for overeating is an automatic and inevitable part of any addictive desire. Just aim to notice the justification you give yourself when you are about to overeat. If you find it difficult to identify, delay satisfying your addictive desire for a while and it will become more urgent, like somebody trying to attract your attention.

You might notice more than one justification at a time, and you probably use a few over and over again. These few are your favourites; convincing, reasonable standbys you can always count on to get the food into your mouth.

▸ There may be no limit to the ways addictive overeating can be justified. You might think, for example, 'This is just how I am, someone with no willpower who eats everything in sight.' Or maybe you're fond of telling yourself, 'Just one little bite won't make any difference.' It's amazing how much you could eat with this one!

▸ Managing your addictive desire to eat can take place in the supermarket, when you walk down the aisles and hear your favourite goodies calling out to you. In a sense, you make a choice to eat those foods when you choose to buy them. If you don't buy them, you won't be eating them.

‣ If you buy certain food 'for others' but usually end up eating it yourself, be honest with yourself about that, and choose what you really want to do. It's fine to leave it there in the shops, and you're more likely to do that if you remember you can always come back for them another day.

‣ If you often buy addictive food for others, you might want to ask yourself why you are doing that. Do you really want to perpetuate this problem in your own community or start to solve it? See if you can find healthier options to offer your family and friends. Healthier options usually don't have that addictive 'kick' to them, so they aren't as attractive and compelling, but maybe it's time for all of us to get smarter about this.

‣ If lack of money is your favourite justification for eating manufactured food, please understand that in terms of nutrition (rather than addiction) you are much better off eating real food. Processing, packaging, advertising and marketing all cost a great deal of money, so that's what you're really paying for. People spend their working lives creating slogans such as '95% fat free' for something that's mostly sugar, and 'made with olive oil' for a sauce that's mostly vegetable oil. Who pays their wages? You?

‣ You've started, so why not continue? If what you've read of this book so far has made sense to you but you haven't put it into practice yet, look to see how you are justifying that. Too busy? Doesn't feel right? Keep forgetting about it? Waiting for someone to do it for you?

LESLEY'S STORY

It's a cliché but it's true to say that I've tried every diet in the book. And they all worked wonderfully. The problem was that I could never stick to any of them for any length of time. I'd start off feeling determined, full of expectations and excitement, believing this to be the one that would finally streamline my massive thighs and hips without leaving me feeling resentful and grumpy from self-denial and hunger.

But within a week or two, usually when I was particularly tired, upset or pre-menstrual, I'd slip back to my old comfort eating, justifying it with a library of personal excuses for why I 'deserved a treat', or 'needed a lift' or whatever. What I hadn't grasped was that as soon as I went on any form of diet I was doomed to failure.

It took a while for it to really sink in and for me to view the whole 'desire' thing as a positive opportunity. I found that the more I looked forward to the addictive desire hitting me, so to speak, in order to confront it and work through it, the less powerful it was. My familiar situations, incidentally, were never physical situations for me, such as craving biscuits with coffee or desert after a meal. It was always emotional states that triggered my desire; whenever I felt particularly tired, fat, fed up, ugly, etc.

And now I truly believe I have the power to face all these negative emotional states without the need to throw high fat, high sugar food into my mouth in order to deal with it. This, for me, is what is so very extraordinary about this approach.

This has quite literally given me back my self-esteem, my ability to choose what to eat and when to eat it, and the freedom to go where I want and do what I want without being afraid of food. Since attending the seminar I have thrown out the thirty or so 'healthy eating' books I had on my shelf and turned my back on dieting forever. I now choose good, nutritious food, I have great self-esteem and I feel really in control of the one area of my life that has caused me so many problems over the years. Oh yes, and I've lost about 30 pounds.

CHAPTER SIX
GIVE YOURSELF A BREAK

So far we've looked at how to change the way you think about eating. With this approach you'll have control at your fingertips – instead of chocolate and cake crumbs! You'll make progress through persistence, and through getting to the truth of your answers to those three questions. You gain greater control as you become more aware of the thinking around these three themes that are driving your behaviour.

However, there are some issues you may bring to this process that can block your progress. When you understand what they are you'll be able to notice and overcome them. Then you continue unhampered, working towards developing more control over what and how much you eat.

The obstacles we'll look at in this chapter are guilt, fear and perfectionism. You might encounter one of these as a problem or two of them or all three. Often they go hand in hand, so you might be dealing with all of them to some extent.

GUILT can be a valuable emotion provided it isn't exaggerated, dragging you down into chronic self-hatred. The reason guilt can be a valuable response to overeating is because it's a sign you're doing something self-destructive. If you wrecked somebody else's health, or if you kept lying or breaking your word to somebody else, you would expect to feel some guilt about that, wouldn't you?

Behaving in that way means that a certain amount of guilt is appropriate. It's telling you something, and if you listen you can see how you want to respond to what it's saying. Part of what rewards you whenever you eat less is the absence of that guilt: greater peace of mind and sense of integrity.

It's very common, though, to take that appropriate amount of guilt about overeating and exaggerate it out of all proportion, *in an attempt to get yourself to change your ways*. You will know what I'm talking about if you are one of those people who calls themselves dreadful names, who judges themselves so harshly, using words they would never dream of saying to anyone else. This is the bullying tactic I described in Chapter One. It's the way you try to coerce and threaten yourself into submissive compliance: 'Don't you dare step out of line again - or you'll regret it, you ****** ***!' You figure if you can just be nasty enough to yourself, you'll get your act together, be good and follow the rules.

Guilt becomes a serious obstacle when it's severe like this. You can feel guilty most of the time, possibly about pretty much everything, but especially about your eating and almost certainly about your weight. Extreme, unrelenting guilt blocks your progress because it undermines your self-esteem. It takes some effort to change this because you start out with so little confidence in and regard for yourself. Why put effort into creating a better life for yourself if you don't deserve it? Why fight for your life if your life is worthless?

This kind of self-hatred is often strongest when it's directed at body size, keeping you locked into weight loss as the only reason you would want to eat less. Perhaps you improve your eating for a while in an attempt to lose weight. Maybe you lose a bit and maybe you don't, but your self-hatred persists, so it's easy for your motivation to fade. Then, it's often a case of, 'what the heck, I'm fat and hopeless anyway, so why not go ahead and eat everything I come across'.

It could be that appearance matters to you most because it's what everybody else sees and makes their judgments about. But your harshest judge is likely to be you, and this is what keeps you from making real changes.

If you recognise yourself here, you could be one of those extremely capable people who cover up their self-loathing with an over-committed, people-pleasing lifestyle. You rarely take time for yourself because you always put others first. If someone pays you a compliment, you find some way to invalidate it. If someone steps on your foot, you're the one who apologises. You find it tough to say 'no' and allow yourself to be walked over like a doormat. You rarely think of yourself, only of others. The chances are you've even been reading this book with someone else in mind.

Of course it's not a bad thing to look after people and to put others first. But think of the advice given aboard an airliner in case the cabin pressure drops and oxygen masks are released. Even if you are travelling with your own children: first, you put on your own oxygen mask, then you help others with theirs.

It's really a question of finding a balance. If you rarely attend to your own needs, then that balance is not in your own best interests. It may not even be in the best interests of the people who depend on you.

If this is even close to your style, see if you use that toxic guilt as a stick to beat yourself up. You may fear that if you eased up on the guilt and forgave yourself a bit, you'd never stop eating. But it doesn't work that way – and you know it doesn't, don't you?

Forgiving yourself doesn't make you apathetic. Having some compassion for yourself doesn't mean you then never want anything to change. In fact the reverse is true. If you wanted a child to develop in some way, to face his fears and try something new and challenging, you know instinctively that patience, recognition and unconditional love are what will support that child most. It's exactly the same with the support you give to yourself.

The antidote to exaggerated guilt is forgiveness and compassion. Forgiveness and compassion for yourself come from claiming your essential worth as a human being, from getting in touch with the spirit in you, who exists quite apart from anything you do and anything you happen to look like.

FEAR can come in a number of forms.

FEAR OF FAILURE may be inevitable to some degree, but for many it can seem not so much a fear as a certainty. It could be that overeating has been a part of your life for so long you've resigned yourself to the way things are, giving up even the possibility of real change.

Perhaps at times you go through some half-hearted motions of trying, with a vague sense of, 'I really should do something about this'. Your deep resignation, though, means you won't put anything like enough effort into it. If you really went for it and failed yet again it would be too disappointing, so it's not worth the risk. So you make petty attempts at some superficial changes, fail (of course!) and resign yourself once again to being out of control.

Usually something else gets blamed in this process. It becomes a case of, 'I would have stuck to it, but my family... but my job... but my love of food got in the way.' This is how a fear of failure actually creates failure! It's a self-fulfilling prophecy.

Recognising this fear is a good place to start, so it's helpful to admit that you fear you'll fail. This, of course, requires some courage because you're acting in the face of fear, not in its absence. This is good, and you want to set your sights high enough so that some of your fear of failure appears. Aim high, but not purely in terms of weight loss. Chapter Seven may help you to find some other targets. Then you get involved, putting as much effort and time and energy and attention into it as you can, even in the face of your conviction that it will never work. And guess what will happen then? You'll fail!

Let me explain. You see, there's failure and there's failure, and a certain amount of failure is inevitable. Not only is it to be expected, but failure is a normal, and even essential, part of learning. I was delighted to discover that this idea was made famous by Thomas Edison. Often regarded as the greatest inventor ever, Edison was the first to record sound and took out over 1,000 patents. Most people would regard him as successful.

Throughout it all, he saw failure as an essential part of the process. I can imagine him saying to himself, 'well, that's another way not to make a light bulb... and that's another way...' And so on, until he got it right and the light bulb glowed. His positive relationship with failure was the key to his success. If he had let his failures get on top of him, he wouldn't have got there in the end.

To Edison, failure simply meant that there was something else to learn, and it can mean that to you too. So any time you fail, you either give up trying or you look to see what there is for you to learn. Failure isn't the problem; it's how you respond to failure that determines your success in the long term.

FEAR OF SUCCESS can be just as much of an obstacle for those with low self-esteem. This is because not only will you expect to fail, but failure will seem familiar and safe. Success at anything can be frightening and some people fear they might change too much, in ways they don't like and can't handle. Many very successful people with lower self-esteem sabotage themselves in some significant way, and often this is with overeating or other addictions.

Cope with this fear by taking things as they come, reminding yourself that you always have the freedom to return to overeating. It's up to you: if you don't like being in control of what you eat and all it means, you don't have to stick with it.

It can make a big difference to move your motivation away from appearance and towards health. If all you care about is 'looking good', this can simply reinforce lower self-esteem. Wanting the best of health generates higher self-esteem – because you're worth it, *because you say so*. Both are no doubt involved in your choices about food, but too often appearance dominates.

Prioritize health, and as your self-esteem improves, your tendency to self-sabotage lessens. Higher self-esteem means you become less self-conscious and less sensitive to criticism, you feel more at ease and at more peace with yourself, more creative, productive and enthusiastic about life in general. In other words, you discover in time that there's not really too much to fear.

FEAR OF NATURAL HUNGER often results from years of dieting. Following a diet usually creates a strong sense of deprivation, so whenever natural hunger surfaces, it's met with anxiety and even panic because you believe you're not allowed to satisfy it.

Many people overeat so that they can be absolutely sure they won't feel hungry before they eat again. This makes sense to some extent, but it's very much a matter of degree. If you fear hunger so much that you must never, ever feel it at all, of course you'll find it tough to eat less.

As with any fear, the way to overcome it is by facing it. Make sure some food is available so that you know you are choosing to feel your hunger and how long you will feel it for. It would be best to keep food with you that is nourishing and not as compelling as more addictive food, with sugar, for example. Then, gradually allow yourself to move towards feeling your natural hunger. You don't need to skip meals in order to do this, but perhaps eat less at your meals or have fewer snacks in between.

Natural hunger isn't a bad thing; it's a signal to eat something soon. It's perfectly normal and natural to feel it sometimes; it comes and goes, and it's not completely unpleasant. (If it's physically painful, it would be wise to consult a health professional about that.) As much as you can, discover the difference between natural hunger and your addictive desire to eat. This can take time, and as we've already seen it's not completely reliable, but it can be valuable to identify natural hunger and be willing to feel it sometimes.

FEAR OF THE ADDICTIVE DESIRE TO EAT is very common because the desire can seem to overwhelm you and force you to overeat, despite your best efforts. This means you are likely to fight it and find it impossible to accept. As we saw in Chapter Three, when you fight it, it fights back, so the more you want it to go away, the more it's going to be there and the more it will seem to be a problem.

You can overcome this fear if you remember that your feeling of desire doesn't make you overeat. You overeat because you want that feeling of unsatisfied desire to go away. Whenever you do some addictive eating, your desire becomes satisfied at some point, and then it's gone, at least for a while. You feel 'normal' again, but you've just gone through another binge.

By letting yourself accept your feeling of desire, you gain the ability to be in control. While you feel this desire, you are not overeating as a direct result – and if you keep this in mind you will be able to overcome your fear of it.

If you're afraid of something in the dark, you can turn on a light. Shine a light on your unsatisfied, addictive desire to eat and take a good look at it. When you do you'll see there are no monsters there, but just an uncomfortable feeling, which will pass in time.

PERFECTIONISM could be the way you think about almost everything, certainly more than just about food. It shows up in those niggling thoughts that no matter what you achieve, you could and should have done better. With food, you either maintain a rigid control of your eating, with not a bite out of place, or you eat in a way that's completely indulgent with no attempt to take any control at all. For a perfectionist, it's all or it's nothing.

Perfectionism makes it impossible to stay motivated long term because any time any one thing is out of place, it's all invalidated. If it's not 100 per cent perfect, it's 100 per cent rubbish. Perfectionists zero in on the one thing that's wrong and that one thing becomes everything. It becomes the evidence that you're not good enough and maybe never will be.

Many perfectionists associate eating 'perfectly' with living 'perfectly'. For periods of time their eating is healthy and in control, and their home is tidy and clean, the bed gets made every day, clothes get picked up and the cat gets fed. Some people will tie in trips to the gym or abstaining from alcohol. Then, one thing goes wrong and it all goes wrong.

For many perfectionists, there's something hugely enjoyable about the 'perfect' phase. It generates a powerful sense of exhilaration and energy that's extremely attractive. There's also a downside, though, and that can be an almost constant anxiety that it won't last.

And of course it doesn't last and it never will. It's a very tall order for anyone to stay in control of addictive overeating perfectly. In the first place, it's impossible to define 'perfect eating'. The very idea conjures up silly questions, such as how many peas you need for optimum health.

We can only make our best, educated guesses at what we need to eat each day. Therefore, a definition of addictive overeating can only be approximate. It's only possible to say whether or not you overeat in terms of degree: either 'a great deal' or 'not very much' or somewhere in between.

The biggest problem with perfectionism, though, is that it's usually carried out by denying free choice. A perfectionist way of eating is so rigid that the sense of prohibition is inevitable. Remember from Chapter One that it's possible to comply with restrictions for a while but eventually this way of thinking sets up rebellious overeating, and you are back where you started, or worse.

Keeping to a rigid regime can be very anti-social, inconvenient, stressful and often obsessive. To make matters even worse, after the regime is broken and overeating resumed, it's tough to get back into control precisely because it was so prohibitive and negative. This is a very common cause of procrastinating about making healthy changes in eating.

All you need to do about this is, instead of aiming for 100 per cent perfection, aim for success in terms of degree. Eliminate absolute success and you eliminate absolute failure at the same time.

Get a picture of all the overeating you do when you're in your out of control phase, and call that 100 per cent addictive eating for you. If you then ate 10 or 20 per cent of that, that would be a pretty good result, wouldn't it? That's what you want to aim for. Then you can say, for example, 'I'm successfully in control of my eating about 80 per cent of the time'. Which is a lot better than nothing! Then you can acknowledge your success; so then you can stay motivated.

Simply stop aiming for perfection. *You don't need it in order to succeed*. It's not perfection that leads you to success in the long term. What leads to your success is your ability to deal with your addictive desire to eat. When you have developed that skill, then, even when you do eat in an addictive way, you can easily get back into control. (32, 33)

WHAT YOU CAN DO

‣ Whenever you forgive yourself for some overeating you've done, follow it with an action to back it up. Find a symbolic act of self-nurturing that's a little bit of a challenge. Perhaps you eat some vegetables if you don't often do that, or choose to accept an addictive desire for something sugary. Eating something healthy can be every bit as positive a move in the right direction as not eating something that's bad for your health.

‣ I usually find that those people who feel extremely guilty about eating are not seeing that they've got choices. Guilt is the feeling that goes along with the belief that you're 'not allowed to eat like this.' As you begin to work with the themes in this book, you will begin to see your choices more clearly and so you will be able to make the choices that you are prepared to live with. As a result, guilt lessens.

‣ Find compassion for yourself about overeating by thinking of someone you like, and even admire, who is as large or larger than you. This could be someone you know or someone famous. Consider the real possibility that they struggle with food, privately, in the same way you do: overeating, feeling guilty about it, breaking promises to themselves, failing to make changes over and over again, and loathing the way they look. If you can feel any compassion for them, you could allow yourself to feel some compassion for yourself.

If you can forgive them for their struggle, you can forgive yourself for yours. Paradoxically, this means you are more likely to change, not less.

▸ If you fear being slimmer, camouflage your weight loss. For example, if you fear attention of a sexual nature, wear baggy, less fashionable clothing. Hiding any weight lost will also help you a great deal in prioritizing eating for health.

▸ Let go of black-and-white, all-or-none thinking, thinking instead in terms of shades of grey or percentages. Aim for 80 per cent, or whatever seems to work for you. If that's too high, aim for 50 per cent and keep looking for ways to improve on that.

▸ Be willing to give up the excitement of perfection. Whenever you are in one of your 'perfect' phases, I suggest you deliberately eat in a way that's imperfect. Mess it up, here and there. You'll lose the thrill of the perfection, but (provided you're managing your addictive desire) you'll also lose those plunges into the nightmare, out of control eating when it all falls apart. Know that 'perfect' eating really is unnecessary, either for weight loss or optimum health.

Whenever you have been 'imperfect' notice what justification you give yourself the next time you feel your addictive desire. It's likely to be a very familiar, 'I've already blown it so I might as well overeat'. When you refuse to buy into that justification, you break that cycle of all-or-nothing. This is how you develop the skill of eating less in an imperfect way.

▸ What percentage of success did you have with your eating today? Acknowledge one thing you did or didn't eat that you are pleased about.

MAGGIE'S STORY

There have been many benefits I've received from doing this seminar, but there's one that surprised me and this one has been a real joy. The reason it surprised me is because I had become so accustomed to the constant complaining in my head, a sort of whining to myself in the background or sometimes in the foreground of my thoughts, but never going away for very long. I was continually moaning to myself about what I ate and how I looked and how it wasn't at all like I wanted it to be.

It was like going through life with someone whispering in your ear, 'you're a failure' every minute of every day. It was only when I noticed it had gone that I realised it had been there, if you know what I mean. I don't think it's gone completely, I should say, but it's quite different now.

I did not like the idea of eating being an addiction, so that took some getting used to. It seemed much too judgmental and harsh. But it did give me a way to get out of this mental whining that things are not like how you want them. It comes down to that fact that you can't continue to justify overeating and stop overeating at the same time.

It sounds so obvious now that I'm writing this down, but that's what you really want, isn't it? You want the best of both worlds: overeating without any of the bad consequences. So the thing was to ask myself if this really is the way I wanted to live, and am I likely to get the consequences I'd want to live with later on.

The thing I find most helpful is planning your meal before you start eating and I always do this with my evening meal. I have a little conversation with myself, checking if this really is what I want to eat and how much. I'm clear about it before I start eating and then I can be clear about it when I've stopped, because I always want to go on after I've finished. So then I think, that's what the addiction wants to eat, it's not what I want.

CHAPTER SEVEN
GOOD FOOD AND BAD FOOD

Whenever you come across any information on nutrition, there are two problems you're likely to encounter: a lack of trust and a lack of fun. The lack of trust comes from all the confusing advice that seems to change so fast it makes you dizzy. Then, you're told to stop eating the food you enjoy most, so it all boils down to nothing more than another nasty, boring diet.

This loss of trust and fun can work together so that you don't take any nutritional advice too seriously and continue to get more fun out of eating.

I know there's something about this that isn't working for you or you wouldn't be reading this book, so take heart. Research on nutrition in the past decade has been phenomenal, and it has certainly been a mighty challenge to keep up with it. Everyone has been on a huge learning curve, and it's really to be expected that we're still in a process of discovery in this extraordinarily complex field.

I suggest three strategies, which you'll need all together: develop and maintain an attitude of free choice; try different styles of eating to see what works for you; and get to know your addictive desire for the food you don't need.

1. AN ATTITUDE OF FREE CHOICE   It could be that seriously considering any dietary advice threatens to prohibit your addictive overeating. It seems that taking it on means you'll be depriving yourself of your treats.

This means that the advice, *no matter what it is*, is likely to be challenged, denied, ignored or persistently compromised in hundreds of ways. For example, thinking a limp slice of green pepper on a pepperoni pizza is a portion of vegetables!

Nutritional information can be useless without a good sense of choice. People with a poor sense of their own freedom of choice about food will eat something knowing it will make them ill. They will even eat food they don't particularly enjoy, and maybe food that's gone bad. They feel compelled to do that because of their rebellion against their imagined prohibition.

When discovering nutritional information, there is absolutely no need at all to think in terms of restrictions and prohibitions. Think instead of different choices creating different outcomes. Change this attitude, and the magic starts to happen.

2. TRY DIFFERENT STYLES OF EATING If, for example, you feel tired a lot of the time, you could cut down on sugar in all its forms to see if you end up with more energy. It's possible you could see a difference within a day or two. Or, if you've been suffering with acid indigestion, arthritis or headaches, it might be worth cutting out wheat and rye to see if that will make any difference. You might see an improvement within days or at the most a few weeks. (34)

Take ideas such as these as experiments, and if there's no benefit you can always go back to your old ways. If you get a good result, you take that feedback and you bring that into the way you make your own choices. If you don't experiment you might never have the feedback you need.

If you make choices to eat certain kinds of food, you get a certain kind of outcome. Poor sleep, for example, or constipation, feeling bloated or lethargic. If you make different choices, all of this can change. Your body works better, and you feel less stressed, more mentally alert and more at peace with yourself.

Nutritional information gives you good clues as to what these experiments might be, to create and notice the different outcomes. The choices you make have cumulative effects, so that you can feel better and better (or worse and worse) over time. If you appreciate the better health and self-esteem you will lose weight, assuming you're overweight to start with. But you'll be achieving it in a way that's empowering and sustainable.

It's possible, though, that you've already got some of that feedback. I've had many conversations with clients who seem to suddenly remember how wonderful they felt on some diet they were on years ago. It could easily be that it was simply because they weren't eating so much sugar or perhaps wheat, but all they cared about at the time was the weight. Either they didn't lose enough or it didn't last, so they threw the baby out with the bath water.

This strategy will work best if you try different styles of eating based on the best nutritional advice you can find; otherwise your intervention won't be much more than a stab in the dark. For example, it won't make sense to try eating nothing but ice cream because there's no nutritional basis for such a strategy.

A good principle is to go for foods that are rich in nutrients. In other words, a wide variety of food that is close to its natural state (not manufactured), and mostly vegetables. (35, 36, 37)

It is now thought that the majority – maybe two-thirds of our population – would do best to consume far fewer starchy carbohydrates such as sugars and grains. This doesn't necessarily mean 'low-carb' because there are carbohydrates in vegetables and fruit.

If you don't see any benefit from the changes you've made, it will be tough to continue because it will seem a huge effort for little or no reward. Remember from

Chapter Two that losing weight isn't the best motivation, in part because it's a slower process. The improvements in mood, energy, sleep, digestion and self-esteem that come from eating in healthier ways give you much faster and more direct feedback. It's also feedback that's just as relevant after you've lost weight, and that's crucial.

3. KNOW YOUR ADDICTIVE DESIRE   This is your desire or appetite for food you don't need, either in terms of quantity or quality. There's no need to aim to stop feeding your addictive desire entirely, just go for less often, but in order to do that you need to be able to identify it in the first place.

As we saw in Chapter Three, addictive desire is triggered by cues based on your past experience. Your desire is your expectation of eating, and along with that release of dopamine in your brain, it triggers the release of appetite hormones, including insulin. In other words, it can feel like hunger – even at the end of a meal.

Addictive desire can also have a profound influence on your preferences, especially if you tend to eat manufactured foods. As a general principle, most food created outside the home will sell better if it has an addictive quality to it. This means it is likely to contain sugars, wheat and poor quality oils that your brain experiences as more rewarding, pleasurable or satisfying. When you've been eating those foods for a while, *you come to expect that level of reward as normal*. And this means that eating something natural such as green, leafy vegetables feels like a nasty shock.

This is why making changes to eat in healthier ways can initially seem hugely unattractive and no fun at all. However, it doesn't take long to adjust and for your taste buds to adapt. When you no longer overwhelm your system with artificial products, you will find you're more able to appreciate the enormous range of flavours and textures available in real food.

What doesn't automatically adapt is the way you're thinking. The key is in accepting that real food is not going to have quite the same addictive, compelling and exciting quality to it.

It's important to enjoy your food, but if enjoyment is your only consideration, you are likely to be eating in an addictive way. Remember you always have free choices about what you eat, and choose the outcome you are willing to live with. Overeating can be fun, but improved health and self-esteem can be profoundly rewarding alternatives.

For me, it's also about accepting some degree of humility, in that I'm not in charge of how the universe works. I'm not indestructible. I live in a body that is part of nature. Gravity is beyond my control, so it's best for me to live with my body in a way that takes gravity into considera-tion. There can be a degree of arrogance in the view that we should be able to eat anything at all and retain the best of health.

Even if you're not so interested in living past 100, the quality of your life is in large part determined by the quality of the food you eat. The food you eat and don't eat, as much as anything else, will determine the length of time you stay in good health, able to do what you want to do in life, have some independence and be free from pain and disease. *It is completely realistic to expect to go through your old age feeling strong and in good health.*

The only time it's too late to make changes is when you're dead. Assuming you're not dead, you can begin to improve your health and your chances of staying healthy by choosing what you eat on a daily basis, and, of course, keeping active.

Many people believe there's no such thing as good food and bad food. All of it is fine, they say, so long as you don't eat too much of any one thing. This is the way they justify their addictive overeating. Now you know better. See if your idea of a wide variety is in fact a wide variety of sugar, processed grains and poor quality oils – all combined, flavoured and packaged in different ways.

WHAT YOU CAN DO

▸ Do you see how there's no need to think in terms of prohibition? Just notice what results come from what particular food choices, and make the effort to remember that the next time you're faced with similar decisions.

▸ Eat real food in order to build lean mass, which is every bit as important as losing fat. This is why it's better to think in terms of 'leaning out' rather than 'losing weight' – because the weight you don't want to lose is your lean mass.

▸ Eat in a way that keeps oxidative stress at a minimum by increasing those foods that deliver antioxidants (especially vegetables) and decreasing manufactured foods that increase free radical levels through the process of their metabolism.

▸ Eat in ways that reduce the systemic, low-level inflammation that's behind a huge range of diseases. For example, saturated and omega-3 fats are anti-inflammatory, while seed and vegetable oils are inflammatory. For many people, wheat and rye irritate the gut wall, contributing to an inflammatory response in the body.

▸ Educate yourself. For example, seed and vegetable oils damage cell membranes, making every cell in the body less efficient. Trans fats found in hydrogenated oils are well known to wreak all kinds of havoc in the body.

▸ When making choices, know that sugar drains energy from the body, so think of sugar as *the opposite of food*. The single best thing you can do for your health may be to reduce your sugar intake. Your body may regard many carbohydrates as sugar, so that cereals and breads have a similar effect on you as table sugar.

▸ If chocolate is your thing, have you thought about improving the quality of what you buy? Chocolate itself can be beneficial, but not when tiny amounts are mixed together with very poor quality fats and refined sugar, as is the case with most popular commercial bars and sweets. You could accept your addictive desire for the endless fixes of flavoured, sugary fat and save your money for more occasional, top-quality brands with a much higher percentage of dark chocolate.

It's not nearly as addictive, so you may find it easier to eat in a controlled way. This also means that your preference is likely to be for the more sugary versions – which has nothing to do with chocolate itself.

RUBY'S STORY

I'm an accountant, not a writer, so I hope this makes sense. I still want to lose weight but these are the benefits I'm getting right now and I can hardly believe how thrilled and excited I am with them. Weight loss is great but it's certainly not the whole picture any more, not even the biggest part of it.

Better skin condition. No more frequent sore throats due to a weak immune system. Ability to breathe easily. Less risk of a heart attack or cancer. Less risk of varicose veins, which runs in my family. No more hair loss due to poor nutrition. Feel like a cat (all stretched and supple) when I wake up, instead of bloated. No more shame (that inability to look the shopkeeper in the eye when I buy sweets). No more hiding what and how much I eat. No more roller coaster eating and the emotions attached to it. I can eat sweets if I want to, any time and any amount, they will still be there tomorrow and the diet doesn't start then. No more fear of going out with friends because it might ruin my diet. No more boring my friends with my weight problems and diet stories.

I can stare down a cookie. I control food, it doesn't control me. The invisible monster really doesn't exist. No more waking up every morning in a state of fear and panic, wondering if I'm going to stick to my diet that day.

I noticed an interesting justification this morning. I woke up and decided that since it's my birthday, I'll have cookies and tea to celebrate. This was at 6am in the morning. Then I realised that I don't have to justify it! I decided it's fine, reached for the cookie jar and suddenly didn't feel like it. This is probably my first birthday ever that I am not stuffing my face with cake!

There was a box of chocolates in the office the whole day. I decided to eat four, had them, enjoyed them, and the box never bothered me for the rest of the day.

[Author's Note: Ruby wrote this for the first edition of this book, soon after she attended one of my seminars. She emailed me six years later to say: *"My eating is still under control. I overeat sometimes but to be honest when it happens I'm not even too worried. I've kept off the 35 pounds, without any dieting."*]

CHAPTER EIGHT
PUTTING IT ALL TOGETHER

Surely the worst thing about starting a diet is that sense of committing yourself to it. No matter what the diet is, there's going to be some kind of restriction in food type, calories, points or whatever, and the idea is that you're now going to be following this for the foreseeable future. You might try not to think about it, but somehow you're unable to ignore that there'll be no more overeating, or no more eating those particular things you love.

You wonder how long you can keep it up. If you do keep it up, you don't get to eat those things or in those quantities. But if you don't keep it up, *you've failed again*. It looks like a no-win situation.

There's an excellent solution to this, and once adopted it's empowering and it's effective. The way to think about this is to only make choices about what you will or won't eat just for the present time, and not to make any assumptions or predictions about the future as far as overeating is concerned.

I say as far as overeating is concerned, because you might want to make future choices by thinking, for example, that you'll buy something to have for dinner tomorrow night. You could be someone who shops once a week, so of course you're going to be making many predictions about what you'll be eating in the future. But when you encounter your addictive desire to eat – between meals perhaps or after a meal or while watching TV in the evening – you can only say for sure whether or not you'll accept that desire in that present moment.

It makes such a big difference to let go of any assumptions about your excess, addictive eating. You simply don't know if you will, in the future, eat considerably more food than you need. And the wonderful thing is, you don't need to know.

To start with, this can seem frightening because it's likely you'll lack confidence in this method. You'll understandably want to feel comforted by a guarantee of success. But it's recognizing real freedom of choice whenever you experience your addictive desire that is so liberating because it eliminates any sense of deprivation. If you let yourself know that certain food or quantities of food will always be available to you – tomorrow, next week, whenever – it will be much, much easier to pass on them today.

Develop the skill of making your choices as you go. All you need to do is choose which outcome you want to create for now, remembering the complete picture, including the downside as well as the upside. In time those choices can certainly add up. You will either have made more choices to eat in ways that will age your body faster or in ways that will keep you younger for longer.

If you wake up in the morning worried about whether you'll fall off the wagon today, just remember that you have no way of knowing, because you can only deal with your addictive desire to eat at the time it's happening. Then, you can go though the moments of your day *with the intention of noticing your addictive desire to eat as it occurs.*

At first you might not notice every time, and find that you go ahead and eat in an addictive way without even realising. This is okay, because just noticing some of your moments of desire is something you can build on over time.

However, even when you've noticed that you're experiencing an addictive desire, there's still the question of whether or not you will satisfy it. If you have rarely, or perhaps never, given a second thought to that, it can take a huge effort at first to get those brain cells working in a different way. As we saw in Chapter Four, two distinct areas of your brain need to connect and communicate in order to make this as effective as possible.

Our brains respond to the ways we think, so if you've spent substantial time in your life reacting unconsciously to your desire, it will take a strong intention on your part to turn that around. Most importantly, you can only do this while you are experiencing your addictive desire to eat. Once you start that ball rolling, though, it becomes easier the more you do it. At first it can feel like being stuck between a rock and a hard place – just know that the hard place does become softer!

Know that you don't *have to* do any of this, ever, so that you know this desire isn't being forced upon you. You can continue to overeat all your life, and even if you stopped doing that, you can always return to it. It's when you deny that freedom that you'll find yourself hoovering up everything in sight, fearing this could be your last indulgence. When food is forbidden – or about to be forbidden – you've absolutely got to eat it all right now because this may be your last chance. By leaving future options open, you'll be far less likely to procrastinate, to continue to put off making any changes at all.

In dealing with my addictive desire to eat, I've found it helpful to take into consideration that I'm living in a bizarre environment as far as food is concerned. This is a culture where intelligent and creative people are paid good money to convince me to eat food that will make me ill. Meanwhile, other intelligent and creative people are paid good money to make that food as available, tasty and attractive as possible.

We can easily see the impact our environment can have on us by looking at the many examples of dramatic changes in food culture. Traditional cultures created leaner populations; in Japan, Africa and the Pacific Islands, as just a few examples. As the cultures changed, often because increased wealth attracted the modern food industry, populations became more overweight and obese.

There are many examples of people who moved from one culture to another and the same thing happened. In their traditional culture, the Japanese have the lowest rates of heart disease and are among the longest-lived people in the world. Those who migrate to America, though, become overweight and get heart disease just as much as other Americans.

In all these cases, an environment dominated by manufactured food has lead not only to excess weight, but also to what are known as the diseases of civilization: high blood pressure, bone, muscle and joint strains, most cancers, autoimmune diseases, diabetes and heart disease.

This shows clearly the impact of modern culture, with its constant supply of attractive but toxic food, on weight and health. Of course you were born with genes that influence what type of disease may manifest itself in your body. But it's how you live that determines how and when these genes express themselves.

These examples also show that it's not likely that unresolved emotional trauma is the main cause of overeating either. It's not likely that a more affluent culture made populations less capable of dealing with their emotions, or with deep emotional issues they wanted to avoid. What makes much more sense is having easy access to enormous quantities and varieties of highly addictive rubbish. These days we are surrounded by it.

A good principle to remember is that if it's advertised and marketed, it's probably addictive. Anything addictive will sell best; which is why sugars, wheat and fats are inevitably included in these processed foods. We live in a society that has made addictive overeating seem normal, and a great many people place a naive degree of trust in the food industry. Look at how much manufactured, processed food you consume, and if it's much more than a few bites here and there, you may be doing just that.

Our language makes it difficult to see, because we simply don't have ways to describe what's happened to the things we eat over the last couple of decades. Even the phrase 'junk food' includes the word 'food'. It's not food, and far from being benign, these products harm your body. They make you ill, slowly, in much the same way as cigarettes make smokers ill.

An addictive relationship with food isn't something that goes away completely, but it is something you can learn to deal with so that it becomes much less of a problem. Most people try to control their eating by trying to avoid feeling tempted. They buy into the promise of The Magic Cure, which means they'll never encounter an unsatisfied addictive desire. But this means that you never learn how to manage your desire to overeat and you never resolve your conflict with it. And that means you're very likely to relapse.

If you've employed avoidance strategies in the past, you certainly can end up thinking you're a hopeless failure. But all it means is that you haven't yet developed the essential skill of managing your addictive desire to eat. Maybe you didn't know how to do that before you came across this book, but now you do. You stop fighting it and allow yourself to feel it; you resolve the conflict it presents by being willing to accept that uncomfortable, unsatisfied feeling because it's the way you stop eating so much. Know that the feeling of desire could save your life.

This isn't an easy thing to do. Let's face it, if it was, more people would be happy with their eating, their health and their weight, wouldn't they? The thing to remember is that it gets easier in time if it's handled correctly. At first, though, there can be significant conflict to work through. Nobody can ever do that for you, but it is possible to do.

The challenge of facing up to your addictive desire can take time, effort and energy. But balance this against the years of difficulties you may have been living with – let alone potential problems that could lie ahead – and you may find it's well worth the effort.

WHAT YOU CAN DO

▶ Dip into this book from time to time to remind yourself of the things you've discovered here. You might want to mark passages or write notes for yourself in a journal.

▶ Stay involved. Most things in life require maintenance. You don't go to work just one time to have a career. And you don't speak to someone just once in order to have a relationship with them. Why should your relationship with food be any different?

You've now discovered the ways of thinking that get you stuck, traps that mean you're unable to make lasting changes in your eating habits. It's not that you don't fall into these traps ever again, it's that you develop the skill of getting out of them fast. You get skilled at readjusting your frame of mind.

▶ Are you overweight to the extent that it's considered a health risk or simply in a way that's unfashionable? Trying to maintain a fashionably skinny body can bring an extra level of difficulty in maintaining control of overeating.

Whenever you see models in magazines or fashion shows, remember that they weigh less than the clinical criteria for anorexia nervosa. Many, perhaps most, have eating disorders, which means that food is a source of distress for them.

‣ If you are a parent, please note that this book is written for adults, and not for children. It may not be wise to expect children to make adult choices as children's brains aren't capable, and nor should they be. Children need to have some choices made for them and, most importantly, good role models to follow.

SALLY'S STORY

I'm 39, I'm married and I have always worked as a fashion buyer, which I absolutely love. I used to diet a lot when I was in my teens and twenties and that seemed to work quite well, but over the last ten years or so I found it impossible to diet and I ended up feeling rather despondent about it all. I thought that the 'Eating Less' seminar would help me to get back to dieting again, but I think it's been better than that.

This seminar to me was proof to me that I could do something I always had wanted: to make some kind of change so that dieting became unnecessary. I always knew it was a mind thing as much as anything else, but the seminar helped me to see a lot of things more clearly. In particular, looking at the problem of these two incompatible things: knowing you want to eat better, to eat more fruit and vegetables, and you're absolutely convinced in your mind that you'd feel so much fitter and better, and then half an hour later you're eating the wrong thing. Just because you've just got to have that slice of cake or whatever.

Resolving the conflict between this is something most

people don't even begin to do. It's about knowing that by eating better you're actually taking care of yourself. That for me was the essence of the seminar. I do eat much better now, and especially I eat more fruit and vegetables.

I've learned to deal with all the comments about the lost weight, but people seem to have settled about it now and I can just carry on in peace. Although I am aware that I need to keep making an effort with regard to what and when I eat, and although I am sometimes more successful than others, I've really stopped seeing food as anything other than my friend, which is a breath of fresh air!

I go through phases where I eat nothing but fruit until the late afternoon and that works well for me. I wouldn't have been able to do that before I did the seminar. I go though quite long periods of not eating wheat. It goes in phases. I'm more in tune with what food does to my body now. If I snack on bread and honey I'll get very sleepy half an hour later, and a big meal at lunchtime will do the same thing. I feel bloated after I eat white bread.

I hardly ever eat chocolate now because I don't really enjoy it nearly as much as I think I will. Every now and then I go and buy a chocolate bar, maybe once every few months, and I think 'I want it, so I'm going to have it'. But then I eat it and I think that wasn't such a big deal. I don't feel guilty about it. I think I'm less hung-up on food now, which is very nice.

FURTHER HELP

Visit my web site at eatingless.com for current details of products and services to support the material in this book.

BOOKS BY GILLIAN RILEY

All of these are available through bookshops and online booksellers:

Eating Less: Say Goodbye to Overeating

Random House UK/Vermilion (1998, 2005) Paperback and Kindle.

This is my full version, double the length of *Ditching Diets*. It covers similar material, containing more information on research, written exercises to help integrate these ideas, and more detailed instructions on techniques.

How To Stop Smoking And Stay Stopped For Good

Random House UK/Vermilion (1992, 1997, 2007) Paperback and Kindle.

Stopping smoking can be an important part of the process for some of those who overeat. Overeating issues don't get fully addressed while smoking continues.

Willpower!
Random House UK/Vermilion (2003) Paperback and Kindle.
This book covers similar material, but includes general discussions about addictive behaviours, current thinking and research.

Quitting Smoking
Gill & Macmillan/Newleaf (2001) Paperback.
This is my short, easy-read, pocket book version.

BOOKS BY OTHER AUTHORS

Diet 101: The Truth About Low Carb Diets
    (Technion, 2012) Jenny Ruhl
Perfect Health Diet (Scribner, 2012)
    Paul Jaminet, PhD and Shou-Ching Jaminet, PhD
Escape the Diet Trap (Fourth Estate, 2012)
    John Briffa, MD
The Paleo Solution (Victory Belt, 2010)
    Robb Wolf
Wheat Belly (Rodale, 2011)
    William Davis, MD
The End of Overeating (Rodale, 2009)
    David A. Kessler, MD
The Happiness Trap (Robinson, 2008)
    Russ Harris, MD
Rewire Your Brain (Wiley, 2010)
    John B. Arden, PhD

REFERENCES

1. "Binge eating disorder and the night-eating syndrome." A Stunkard, R Berkowitz *International Journal of Obesity* 1996; 20, 1-6
- In this study of 50 obese women diagnosed with Binge Eating Disorder, the frequency of binge eating episodes fell by a massive 72 per cent over four weeks of placebo 'medication'.

2. "Leptin reverses weight loss-induced changes in regional neural activity responses to visual food stimuli." M Rosenbaum, M Sy *Journal of Clinical Investigation* 2008; 118(7), 2583-2591
- This study of a pharmaceutical used a placebo for comparison, and found the placebo had a very powerful effect on leptin levels.

3. "Mind over milkshakes: Mindsets, not just nutrients, determine ghrelin response." AJ Crum, WR Corbin, KD Brownell, et al *Health Psychology*, 2011; 30(4), 424-9
- When volunteers were told that their low-calorie milkshake was high-calorie, the effect on their ghrelin matched the effect that would have taken place if the shake had in fact contained double the calories. It was their expectation - their state of mind - that created this effect.

4. "Do not eat the red food! Prohibition of snacks leads to their relatively higher consumption in children." E Jansen, S Mulkens, A Jansen *Appetite* 2007; 49, 572-577
- Prohibition of snacks that had been coloured red subsequently leads to greater consumption and enjoyment, compared to identical snacks not previously forbidden.

5. "Dieting, perceived deprivation, and preoccupation with food."
GM Timmerman, EK Gregg *Western Journal of Nursing Research*
2003; 25(4), 405-418
- This study found that how much someone feels deprived has
nothing to do with how much they have consumed. Feeling
deprived was seen in this study of 121 women as the major
obstacle to diet maintenance.

6. "Parenting styles and overweight status in first grade." RE
Kyung, JC Lumeng *Pediatrics* 2006; 117, 2047-2054
- Children with authoritarian parents were found to be five times
more likely to be overweight. The parenting style was not
thought to be a reaction to the child being overweight in the first
place.

7. "Perceived deprivation, restrained eating and susceptibility to
weight gain." JT Markowitz, ML Butryn *Appetite* 2008; 51, 720-
722
- These researchers suggest that feeling deprived relates, not to
how much food is eaten, but to thinking in terms of 'limiting the
foods they let themselves eat.'

8. *Why Zebras Don't Get Ulcers* (W. H. Freeman, 1994) Robert
M. Sapolsky, PhD - page 187
- A number of studies have looked at reactions of both animal
and human subjects in stressful situations, and found that the
degree of stress experienced is vastly reduced when there is an
opportunity to escape from or somehow control whatever is
causing the stress. This opportunity isn't necessarily taken; the
fact that there is an option is what makes the difference. In his
landmark book on stress, Dr Sapolsky calls this 'an extraordinarily powerful variable in modulating the stress-response' and
that 'the exercise of control is not critical; rather, it is the belief
that you have it.'

9. "Appearance versus health: does the reason for dieting affect dieting behavior?" E Putterman, W Linden *Journal of Behavioral Medicine* 2004; 27(2), 185-204
- Of the 196 dieters in this study, those who mainly wanted to improve their appearance were more likely to lose control of their eating than those who mainly wanted to support their health.

10. "Naturalistic weight-reduction efforts prospectively predict growth in relative weight, onset of obesity among female adolescents." E Stice, RP Cameron, JD Killen, et al. *Journal of Consulting and Clinical Psychology* 1999; 67(6), 967-74
- This study of 692 young women over four years found that those who dieted and exercised in order to control their weight were more likely to become obese years later.

11. "How can drug addiction help us understand obesity? The addicted human brain: insights from imaging studies." ND Volkow, RA Wise *Nature Neuroscience* 2005; 850), 555-560.
- This paper describes adaptations in the brain that result from repeated rewards, whether drugs or food.

12. "Opioids as facilitators of feeding: can any food be rewarding?" PK Olszewski, J Alsio, et al. *Physiology and Behavior* 2011; 104(1): 105-10
- The answer is yes, although the most rewarding foods are those high in carbohydrates and fats.

13. "Aspects of eating behaviors 'disinhibition' and 'restraint' are related to weight gain and BMI in women." NP Hays, SB Roberts *Obesity* 2008; 16(1), 52-58
- This study of 535 women over 20 years found that the most significant cause of weight gain was eating in response to 'everyday cues'.

14. "Similarity between obesity and drug addiction as assessed by neurofunctional imaging." G-J Wang, ND Volkow, et al *Journal of Addictive Disorders* 2004; 23(3), 39-53
- Dopamine release in the midbrain creates our experience of desire; the release of opioid peptides creates our experience of pleasure when we eat.

15. "A comparison of acceptance- and control-based strategies for coping with food cravings: An analog study." EM Forman, KL Hoffman, et al *Behavior Research and Therapy* 2007; 45, 2372-2386
- Volunteers were instructed either to distract themselves from their cravings or to accept them. Especially when cravings were stronger, acceptance resulted in significantly less distress, frequency and intensity. Acceptance also made it much easier not to satisfy the craving.

16. "Appetite: Measurement and manipulation misgivings." RD Mattes, J Hollis, et al *Journal of the American Dietetic Association* 2005; 105(5), S87-S97
- This article reviews over 100 studies and concludes that even after years of extensive research, sensations of hunger and fullness have proved difficult to define and even more difficult to associate with real-life eating choices.

17. "External cues in the control of food intake in humans." CP Herman, J Polivy *Physiology and Behavior* 2008; 94, 722-728
- In general, people don't really know when they are hungry or full.

18. "Repeated cue exposure effects on subjective and physio-logical indices of chocolate craving." D Van Gucht, D Vansteenwegen, et al. *Appetite* 2008; 50, 19-24
- Craving intensity was measured, and not reinforced by eating. Three days later, craving induced under the same circumstances

was seen to have decreased significantly.

19. "Cue exposure in the treatment of resistant bulimia nervosa." J Toro, M Cervera, et al. *International Journal of Eating Disorders* 2003; 34(2), 227-234 and "Cue exposure vs self-control in the treatment of binge eating." A Jansen, J Broekmate, et al *Behavior, Research and Therapy* 1992; 30(3), 235-241
- These are two studies demonstrating the effectiveness of experiencing unsatisfied desire in dealing with binge eating. Highly impressive results were confirmed at one- and two-year follow-up.

20. "Decreased salivation to food cues in formerly obese successful dieters." A Jansen, S Stegerman, et al. *Psychotherapy and Psychosomatics* 2010; 79, 257-258
- Increased salivation in reaction to food cues indicates desire strength. A group who had successfully lost weight showed decreased reactivity, compared to a group who hadn't, and who showed increased reactivity.

21. "Decision making, impulse control and loss of willpower to resist drugs: a neurocognitive perspective." A Bechara *Nature Neuroscience* 2005; 8(11), 1458-1463
- Difficulty controlling addictive behaviours is due to an imbalance in two neural systems: one impulsive (midbrain, roughly in between the ears) and the other reflective (prefrontal cortex, behind the forehead).

22. "Repetitive transcranial magnetic stimulation reduces cue-induced food craving in bulimic disorders." F Van den Eynde, AM Claudino, et al *Biological Psychiatry* 2010; 67(8): 793-5
- When the prefrontal cortex is activated through magnetic stimulation, cravings in binge eaters subside.

23. "Neural activation patterns of methamphetamine-dependent subjects during decision making predict relapse." MP Paulus, SF Tapert, A Marc, et al. *Archives of General Psychiatry* 2005; 62, 761-768
- Using volunteers in a rehab clinic, it was recorded how much each person used their PFC in games that required making choices. Those with greater PFC activity turned out to be those who stayed off drugs, long term, in the real world.

24. "Successful dieters have increased neural activity in cortical areas involved in the control of behavior" A DelParigi, K Chen, AD Salbe, et al. *International Journal of Obesity* 2007; 31, 440-448
- This study involved women who had lost at least 30 pounds and maintained that weight loss for at least a year. Monitoring brain function while they ate a meal, they had greater PFC activity than a control group with no successful weight loss.

25. "Characterization of the decision-making deficit of patients with ventromedial prefrontal cortex lesions." A Bechara, D Tranel D. *Brain* 2000; 123(11), 2189-202
- Patients with physical damage to the PFC are shown to be insensitive to future consequences, both positive and negative, and are primarily guided by immediate prospects.

26. "Willed action and the prefrontal cortex in man." CD Frith, K Friston, PF Liddle, et al. *Proceedings of the Royal Society (London B)* 1991; 244, 241-246
- Activity in the prefrontal cortex was observed during a series of simple tasks only when volunteers chose for themselves, and not when following instructions during similar tasks.

27. "Behavioral and neuroeconomics of drug addiction: competing neural systems and temporal discounting processes." WK Bickel, ML Miller, R Yi, et al. *Drug and Alcohol Dependency*

2007; 90(1), S85-S91
- The midbrain activates with regard to immediate outcomes; the prefrontal cortex for delayed outcomes.

28. "Putting feelings into words." MD Leiberman, NI Eisenberger, SM Crockett, et al. *Psychological Science* 2007; 18(5), 421-428
- Giving a name to a feeling decreases activity in the midbrain while increasing activity in the prefrontal cortex.

29. "Mood states effects of chocolate" G Parker, I Parker, H Brotchie *Journal of Affective Disorders* 2006; 92(2-3), 149-159
- This review of around 80 studies concluded that although eating chocolate can improve mood while being consumed, it's more likely to extend a low mood than to alleviate it.

30. "Pharmacological versus sensory factors in the satiation of chocolate craving." W Michener, P Rozin *Physiology and Behavior* 1994; 56(3), 419-422
- The pharmacological elements of chocolate, delivered in a capsule, were found to have no effect on chocolate craving.

31. "Stress-induced eating in restrained eaters may not be caused by stress or restraint." MR Lowe, TVE Kral *Appetite* 2006; 46, 16-21
- In a cleverly designed study, a group of volunteers was tricked into believing they had worked much harder than a control group. When given a break with access to snacks, the group who believed they had worked harder ate more.

32. "Perfectionistic self-presentation, body image, and eating disorder symptoms." BM McGee, PL Hewitt, SB Sherry, et al. *Body Image* 2005; 2(1), 29-40
- Perfectionism is strongly associated with all kinds of eating disorders. (This is not to suggest you have a 'disorder', just that trying to be perfect introduces a level of difficulty.)

33. "Do 6-year changes in eating behaviours predict changes in body weight?" V Drapeau, V Provencher, et al *International Journal of Obesity and Related Metabolic Disorders* 2003; 27(7), 808-814
- In women, highly restrained dieting is observed to lead to weight gain in the longer term.

34. "Potential role of sugar (fructose) in the epidemic of hypertension, obesity and the metabolic syndrome, diabetes, kidney disease, and cardiovascular disease." RJ Johnson, MS Segal *American Journal of Clinical Nutrition* 2007; 86, 899-906
- Fructose in particular can induce features of metabolic syndrome: fatty liver, insulin resistance, elevated blood pressure, elevated triglycerides, lower HDL cholesterol. And fructose causes problems even under caloric restriction.

35. "Provision of foods differing in energy density affects long-term weight loss." BJ Rolls, LS Roe, AM Beach *Obesity Research* 2005; 13(6), 1052-1060

36. "Five-week, low-glycemic index diet decreases total fat mass and improves plasma lipid profile in moderately overweight nondiabetic men." C Bouche, SW Rizkalla, J Luo, et al. Diabetes Care 2002; 25(5), 822-828

37. "Relation of food and nutrient intakes to body mass." J Stamler, TA Dolecek *American Journal of Clinical Nutrition* 1997; 65, 366S-373S
- These last three studies show that significantly more body fat is lost when people eat foods low in energy density.

3189422R00069

Printed in Great Britain
by Amazon.co.uk, Ltd.,
Marston Gate.